THE SIMPSONS AND SOCIETY

An Analysis of Our Favorite Family and Its Influence in Contemporary Society

by Steven Keslowitz

HATS
OFF™

The Simpsons and Society: An Analysis of Our Favorite Family and Its Influence in Contemporary Society

International Standard Book Number:
1-58736-253-8
Library of Congress Control Number:
2003112266

Published by Hats Off Books™
610 East Delano Street, Suite 104
Tucson, Arizona 85705 U.S.A.
1-888-934-0888 toll free
www.hatsoffbooks.com

In Memory of Bleeding Gums Murphy:
Now that you're gone,
We're singing the blues.

Foreword

During my senior year of high school, my friends and I formed a club entitled "Backrow Inc." We created the club because we all sat in the back row in our band class. In many ways, we were the heart and soul of the band: we wore goofy glasses without lenses to make everyone laugh, made our official "Backrow Inc." sign, and held up flags that read "Go Percussion" when the drummers played well. Soon, other members of the band (those not seated in the back row) began to join our club. Above all else, the common link that all club members shared was our infatuation with *The Simpsons*.

Between us, we knew *everything* there was to know about the series. Every day, we quoted different lines from the series, and invariably burst into laughter. Our senior year in high school was amazing because of the fun we had in band. While we also spoke about basketball, school, and playing music, our friendship was initially formed on our shared interest in *The Simpsons*. Were we fanatics? Maybe — but there's nothing wrong with knowing everything there is to know about what you love. *The Simpsons* made our senior year memorable.

One of my friends once remarked, "We remember quotes from *The Simpsons*, but don't remember what we learned in History class last year. We'll be telling Simpsons quotes to our grandchildren." All of us hope that *The Simpsons* will always live on.

Steven Keslowitz (also known in Backrow Inc. as Robert Douglas)

....The legacy of *The Simpsons* will live on, and..."They'll Never Stop *The Simpsons*."

Dedicated to my mom, dad, and my brother Justin… and of course, my parakeet, Homer.
I love you all…

TABLE OF CONTENTS

Foreword v
Preface 1
Homer Quotes 3
Introduction: *The Simpsons*: More than "Just a Cartoon" 6

Section 1
Chapter 1
Is Homer a Good Father? 13
Chapter 2
Bart: America's Bad Boy? 29
Chapter 3
Marge: Holding the Family Together 41
Chapter 4
Lisa: True Simpson or Potential Future College Student? 45
Chapter 5
To Speak or Not to Speak:
Maggie Simpson vs. Stewie Griffin 49
Chapter 6
C. Montgomery Burns and the Pursuit of True Happiness . 53
Chapter 7
The Practice of Dr. Hibbert vs. the Malpractice of Dr. Nick
(and a Small Dose of Dr. Steve) 59
Chapter 8
The Minor Characters 71
Chapter 9
The Simpsons vs. Other Television Sitcoms 83

Section 2 — Simpsonian Themes: The Simpsons On...
Chapter 10
The Importance of Cartoons in a Contemporary Society 93
Cartoons and Global Politics: Animation as a Source of
Contemporary Commentary on World Affairs 93
Ay Carumba! Simpsonian News and Views 97
Essay # 1
Politics and the Typographic Mind 101
Essay # 2
The Political Television Commercial:
A Shift in Political Discourse 107

Essay # 3
Why American Exceptionalism Should Cease to Exist....... 115
Essay # 4
The Effects of Industrialization on the Worker:
Homer Simpson as the Industrialized Employee................ 121
Essay # 5
A Critical Evaluation of Descartes' Meditation I................. 131

Conclusion.. 137
Bibliography... 143
A Special Message to My Nuclear Family............................ 147
Acknowledgments 148
About the Author... 149

PREFACE

The Simpsons and Society: An Analysis of Our Favorite Family and Its Influence in Contemporary Society examines each member of the Simpson clan and their impact in our everyday lives. By means of a thorough examination of dozens of important *Simpsons* episodes, I have addressed many interesting issues, which include: whether Homer is a good father, whether it is better for Maggie to remain quiet, whether Bart is truly America's "bad boy," and whether Lisa is truly a "Simpson" or closer to a potential college student. And, just for fun, the book also examines the importance of Marge's hair.

Another chapter of this book is devoted to the impact of *The Simpsons* as compared with the influence of other TV sitcoms over the past century. It is here that I discuss the role of the TV husband and TV wife. Furthermore, this chapter includes a comparison between the parenting techniques of Homer and Bill Cosby.

The second section of this volume contains essays that serve to relate *The Simpsons* to diverse areas of American culture. Here, we find what Bart has to say about American Exceptionalism, whether Homer fits the classic role of the industrialized employee, whether Homer agrees with Neil Postman's arguments pertaining to media culture, and much more. There's also a discussion of Descartes' Evil Genius argument as portrayed on an episode of *The Simpsons*.

There are also some other interesting, informative chapters in this volume: an enlightening discussion of Simpsonian

1

politics and news, a thought-provoking analysis of Mr. Burns and his pursuit of true happiness, and a discussion of Dr. Nick's malpractice as compared with the practice of Dr. Hibbert.

The purpose of this book is to make Americans (*Simpsons* fans and everybody else) think about pertinent issues in contemporary society. Parenting, healthcare, and media culture as portrayed on *The Simpsons* may make fans laugh, but it is also important to realize the importance of these issues in our society. *The Simpsons* isn't afraid to comment on these issues, and neither should Americans fear debate. But before we get too serious, just take a moment and give me a Dr. Hibbert chuckle...ah heh heh heh...

HOMER QUOTES

★ "It's better to watch stuff than to do stuff."

★ "All right, let's not panic. I'll make the money by selling one of my livers. I can get by with one."

★ "Television: teacher, mother, secret lover."

★ "And how is education supposed to make me feel smarter? Besides, every time I learn something new, it pushes some old stuff out of my brain. Remember when I took that home winemaking course, and I forgot how to drive?"

★ "Aw, Dad, you've done a lot of great things, but you're a very old man, and old people are useless."

★ "I never apologize, Lisa. I am sorry, but that's just the way I am."

★ "To be loved, you have to be nice to others EVERYDAY! To be hated, you don't have to do squat."

★ "First you don't want me to get the pony, then you want me to take it back. Make up your mind."

★ "I hope I didn't brain my damage."

★ "Heh heh heh! Lisa! Vampires are make-believe, just like elves and gremlins and Eskimos!"

★ "Here's to alcohol: The cause of, and answer to, all of life's problems."

★ "I saw this movie about a bus that had to SPEED around a city, keeping its SPEED over fifty, and if its SPEED dropped, it would explode! I think it was called, The Bus That Couldn't Slow Down."

★ "I'm a white male, age 18 to 49. Everyone listens to me, no matter how dumb my suggestions are."

★ "Marge, it takes two to lie. One to lie and one to listen."

★ "Marge, please. Old people don't need companionship. They need to be isolated and studied so that it can be determined what nutrients they have that might be extracted for our personal use."

★ "Trying is the first step towards failure."

★ "Oh, Lisa, you and your stories......Bart's a vampire, beer kills brain cells. Now let's go back to that...building...thingie...where our beds and TV...is."

★ "Oh, people can come up with statistics to prove anything, Kent. 14% of people know that."

★ "Remember, as far as anyone knows, we're a nice normal family."

★ "This donut has purple in the middle; purple is a fruit."

★ "This perpetual motion machine she made is a joke: It just keeps going faster and faster. Lisa, get in here! In this house, we obey the laws of thermodynamics!"

★ "Yeah, Moe, that team sure did suck last night. They just plain sucked! I've seen teams suck before, but they were the suckiest bunch of sucks that ever sucked! Oh, I gotta go, my damn wiener kids are listening."

★ "They have the Internet on computers now?"

★ "Oh, well, of course, everything looks bad if you remember it."

★ "Here's good news! According to this eye-catching article, SAT scores are declining at a slower rate.... Hey, this is the only paper in America that's not afraid to tell the truth: that everything is just fine."

★ "Boy, everyone is stupid except me."

★ "Homer no function beer well without."

★ FBI agent Scully: "This is just a simple lie-detector test. I'll ask some simple questions and you should answer with yes or no. Do you understand?
Homer: "Yes." [The machine blows up].

★ Bart: What if we don't find anything?
Homer : Then we'll fake it and sell it to the Fox network.
Bart: They'll buy anything.
Homer: Now son, they also do a lot of quality shows...
    ha ha ha... They kill me."

★ "English? Who needs that? I'm never going to England!"

The Simpsons: More than "Just a Cartoon"

"Cartoons don't have any deep meaning, Marge. They're just stupid drawings that give you a cheap laugh."
— *Homer Simpson, "Mr. Lisa Goes to Washington"*

A recent poll taken by the BBC asked respondents who they felt was the "greatest American of all time."[*] Here is the list of online responses as of June 10, 2003:

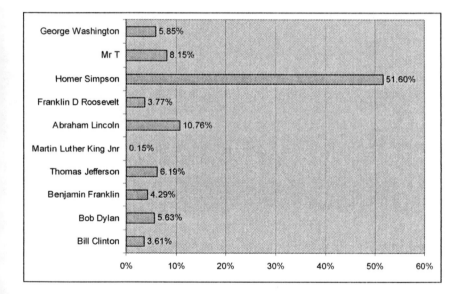

Note that Homer Simpson has over 50% of the votes cast in the Internet poll. Another BBC Internet poll listed Homer as the viewers' choice for favorite U.S. television star.[†] What do these polls say about America and its relationship with *The Simpsons*? Critics of *The Simpsons* would attribute Amer-

[*] Poll results found at: http://newsvote.bbc.co.uk/1/hi/programmes/wtwta/2959462.stm
[†] http://news.bbc.co.uk/1/hi/entertainment/tv_and_radio/2984426.stm

ica's ills (lack of ethics and morality) to the series. However, by responding that Homer Simpson is the most important American of all time, Americans have come to realize that *The Simpsons* directly helps to engender the aura attributed to the United States.

The Simpsons has had the most guest stars of any series of all time. As noted by Michael Solomon in *TV Guide*, "You haven't truly arrived until you merit an appearance on *The Simpsons*."* The guest stars come from all walks of life — from Bret "The Hitman" Hart to Elton John to Stephen Hawking. *The Simpsons* attracts so many guest stars because of its satirical nature: a guest star must expect to be made fun of when they decide to star in a *Simpsons* episode. Still, guest stars often repeatedly star on the show (Kelsey Grammer, for example), because they understand that the show is written extremely well. For example, as Matt Groening stated, "A lot of talented writers work on the show, half of them Harvard geeks. And you know, when you study the semiotics of *Through the Looking Glass* or watch every episode of *Star Trek*, you've got to make it pay off, so you throw a lot of study references into whatever you do later in life."† Guest stars are attracted to *The Simpsons* because it is not an "average" cartoon. Case and point: of all the musicians asked to guest star on the series, only Bruce Springsteen turned down the offer.‡ (Other musicians who did guest star on the series include Brian Setzer, Elton John, Billy Idol, R.E.M., Weird Al Yankovic, Little Richard, Paul McCartney, Ringo Starr, and Mick Jagger, among many others).

World leaders are also attracted to *The Simpsons*: British Prime Minister Tony Blair recently recorded lines for an upcoming episode, and has stated that he enjoys watching

---

* Solomon, Michael. *TV Guide*: Feb. 15-21, 2003, p.27.

† Interview with Matt Groening: http://www.snpp.com/other/interviews/groening93.html

‡ Stated in an interview with Al Jean.

the series. Similarly, John Ashcroft reported on CBS Sunday Morning that he is an avid fan of *The Simpsons*.

The Simpsons Is Pop Culture

Michael Jackson: Hi, I'm Michael Jackson of The Jacksons. Homer: I'm Homer Simpson of The Simpsons.

Homer: WHO IS FONZY!?! Don't they teach you anything at school?

The Simpsons made People Magazine's List of the "200 Greatest Pop Culture Icons"

The Simpsons has transformed the American way of life. Fans of the series view the show as a parody of the "average" American family. Indeed, *The Simpsons* does provide insight into the inner workings of the American household. However, the television audience may not realize that *The Simpsons* has actually shaped our very way of life.

To further examine the aforementioned point, we must explore the impact that the Simpson family has on our lives. For example, Homer's excessive television watching was intended to ridicule the couch potatoes of America. The series has certainly made their point: if you want to be like Homer, watch a lot of television; if you want to be like Stephen Hawking (who guest starred on the series), you better visit the library.

The Impact of *The Simpsons*

While *The Simpsons* often presents allusions to popular movies and television programs, the series has also created its own unique brand of popular culture. *The Simpsons* has satirized the entire Hollywood realm—from Mary Poppins (fans will recall the Shary Bobbins episode) to *The Godfather* to *All in the Family*. While this extensive utilization of satire is a fundamental component to the series, *The Simpsons* would probably be able to survive even if it completely ignored popular culture. The reason for this is that *The Simpsons* has now *become* popular culture. From Bart's bad boy antics to Homer's laziness, the series has become a cornerstone of American life. Case and point: How many times do Americans commonly hear phrases such as "D'oh!" and "Don't have a cow, man" used outside of the series? The language invented on the series coupled with Simpsonian virtues has transformed the very nature of the American familial unit.

Satire in itself has become an American way of life. Any important event that occurs (excluding terrorist activities and mass murders) is immediately ridiculed by television programs and late-night comedians (Jay Leno still hasn't completely stopped talking about O.J.). *The Simpsons* adds an important satirical element to television because it is rare to find a cartoon series in which the main characters voice their opinions about government, politics, or any other matter.

Scholars might scoff at the idea that *The Simpsons* provides true insight into the American way of thinking. However, the following quote from the series serves to buttress my point:

Homer: People will do anything a sign tells them to do.
(He then reads a sign that advertises Duff Beer and drinks a beer.)
Homer: Wow, that really quenched my thirst.
(He then reads another sign for Duff: "Duff Beer: Have Another.")
Homer: ...Or did it [actually quench my thirst]? *(He of course then drinks another beer).*

The above quote speaks directly to the American public, and declares that we as a society are victim to marketing ploys presented by advertisers. I personally will stop and think for a moment the next time I see an ad for Coca-Cola — those sly advertisers might be able to "get" Homer Simpson, but they're not going to "get" me. Thanks, Homer.

In *The Simpsons and Philosophy: The D'oh of Homer*, Paul A. Cantor cites an interesting example of how *The Simpsons* infiltrates the minds of American teenagers.[*] New York Senator Charles Schumer visited a high school to speak about the subject of school violence. One of the students responded to the question of gun control that arose: "It reminds me of a *Simpsons* episode. Homer wanted to get a gun but he had been in jail twice and in a mental institution. They label him as 'potentially dangerous.' So Homer asks what that means and the gun dealer says: 'It just means you need an extra week before you can get the gun.'" In most situations, many fans of *The Simpsons* can relate some aspect of reality to life in Springfield. Often, fans become immersed in the episodes, all the while forgetting that *The Simpsons* is an animated program.

So the next time you think about what features define the "average" American family, look no further than your TV set and watch *The Simpsons*. Television may have been intended to serve as an escape from our real lives, but *The Simpsons* has penetrated the previously impenetrable barrier that separates reality from cartoon. As the series has now reached its 15th season, it is time for us to consider all of *The Simpsons'* noteworthy contributions to American society. They'll Never Stop *The Simpsons*.

There are many reasons that fans of *The Simpsons* have transformed the television series into an institution. (*The Simpsons* licensing constitutes a $1 billion industry.) In the fol-

---

[*]   Cited in *The Simpsons and Philosophy*. Paul Cantor's source: Ed Henry's "Heard on the Hill" column in *Roll Call*, 44, no. 81 (May 13, 1999). Henry's source was the *Albany Times- Union*.

lowing pages, I will discuss why *The Simpsons* is more than just a cartoon. This book will touch upon many aspects of Simpsonian-flavored life in contemporary society: family life, news, politics, and medicine. My goal is to provide the American viewing public with examples of the series' impact on contemporary society. (One quick example: the word "D'oh" was added to the Oxford English Dictionary.) For those of us interested in popular culture, it is important to note that each character in the series represents some aspect of culture in contemporary society. It is to an exploration and analysis of some important Simpson characters that we now turn...

CHAPTER 1

Is Homer a Good Father?

"I'd rather drink a beer than win father of the year."
— *Homer in "Simpsoncalifragilisticexpiala-D'oh-cious,"
the Shary Bobbins episode*

"Ah, aliens! Don't eat me. I have a wife and kids...eat them!"
— *"Treehouse of Horror" episode
in which Homer is abducted by Kang and Kodos.*

Homer as the "Good" Father:
"Everyone else may give up on me, but I know my parents never will."
— *Bart Simpson*

Simpsons fans are well aware of the fact that Homer Simpson is insightful. Each show invariably contains some of Homer's slices of life. For instance, in "Lisa's Pony," Homer lied to Marge but then defended himself by remarking, "Marge, it takes two to lie: one to lie, and one to listen." Funny, but true. Homer's insightful humor almost enables viewers to forget his lack of intelligence — that is, of course, until he does something stupid (like putting nuclear waste on his gums in the "tomacco" episode). However, if we look past Homer's character flaws and witty remarks, we can beg the question of whether or not he is a good father.

First, we must give a definition of a "good" father. A good father is one that is well-intentioned and cares about his children. Homer does have good intentions, and often does care about his three children — when he actually recalls that he has three children. (He often forgets that Maggie exists.) He also does spend many hours of "quality" time with Bart, Lisa, and Maggie on the couch. In contemporary American society, many parents spend most of their time with their kids watching television. Homer can thus be considered the "average" American parent in that he bonds with his kids by means of watching television with them.

Although Homer is generally lazy when it comes to his work, there are times when he works assiduously to provide for his wife and children. For example, in the very first full length *Simpsons* episode ("Simpsons Roasting on an Open Fire"), Homer takes as job as Santa Claus at the mall to obtain money to purchase Christmas gifts for his family. Thus, he demonstrates a fundamental love for his family. In fact, in this episode his love for his family surpasses his penchant for laziness.

In "Lisa's Pony," Homer takes a second job (at the Kwik-E-Mart) because he fears Lisa doesn't love him any more: his plan is to earn enough money to buy her a pony. Of course, he had brought this upon himself: he stopped in for a drink at Moe's and was late to Lisa's saxophone concert. Marge did have to convince him that he should not give up on Lisa. Homer had previously said: "Maybe I should just cut my losses, give up on Lisa, and make a fresh start with Maggie." Obviously, Homer's ignorance often steers him off course. Still, Homer eventually demonstrates his true love for Lisa by sacrificing virtually all of his leisure time in order to try to win her love. Homer stated his new work schedule: "I'll work from midnight to eight, come home, sleep for five minutes, eat breakfast, sleep six more minutes, shower, then I have ten minutes to bask in Lisa's love, then I'm off to the power plant fresh as a daisy." Homer's willingness to give up television in order to win Lisa's love demonstrates that he is a devoted father.

Homer also demonstrates his love for Lisa in the episode entitled "Homr." In the episode, Homer learns that he has had a crayon stuck in his brain since his childhood, and that this has lowered his intelligence. Moe, the unlicensed surgeon in this episode, removes the crayon from Homer's brain. The result is that Homer becomes more intelligent. Homer takes note of his newfound intelligence: "Now, who's up for a trip to the library tomorrow? Notice I no longer say 'liberry' or 'tomorry'." Homer is now better able to understand Lisa's needs, and bonds with her during the short period that he remains intelligent. Just before Homer returns to Moe and asks him to surgically implant the crayon back in his brain, Homer writes the following letter to Lisa: "Lisa, I'm taking the coward's way out. But before I do, I just want you to know: Being smart made me appreciate how amazing you really are." The aforementioned quote serves to emphasize my earlier point: Homer is well-intentioned. He wants to build strong relationships with his children, but his lack of intelligence often does not allow him to do so. However, once he became smart, he truly enjoyed spending time with Lisa.

The Categorical Imperative

In "Homr," Homer certainly demonstrates his love for Lisa. However, Kant's *categorical imperative* would not allow Homer to decide at what times he wishes to bond with Lisa. Instead, Kant would declare that Homer should "Do Y," which in this case should be to bond with his children. He should not bond with his children only when he decides to do so. Still, as mentioned above, Homer is often too ignorant to understand the needs of his children, and thus cannot be held to the standards that Kant sets forth.

Homer's parenting techniques are also examined in "Bart the Daredevil." In this episode, Homer tries to deter Bart from jumping the Springfield Gorge. At the climax of the episode, Homer says the following to Bart: "I tried ordering you, I tried punishing you, and God help me, I even tried reasoning with you."[*] Homer is obviously trying his best to be a good parent in this scene. His efforts take him as far as threatening to jump the gorge himself in order to show Bart how dangerous the jump is. Bart pleads with Homer not to do it and promises never to jump again. Thus, Homer's parenting techniques are completely sound in this scene. Of course, it wouldn't be a *Simpsons* episode without some comedy in this scene. Following Homer and Bart's exchange of words, Homer tells Bart, "You know boy, I don't think I've ever felt as close to you as I do right..." and slips off the cliff. Homer shows that he truly cares about the well being of Bart, and incurs injury as an indirect result of deterring Bart from jumping the gorge.

Other episodes also portray Homer as a good, well intentioned father. In one episode, for example, Homer recalls the time he bought Lisa her first saxophone. At the time, money was tight for the Simpson family, and Homer was saving money in order to purchase an air conditioner. However, he decides to purchase Lisa her first saxophone instead of buying the air conditioner. He demonstrates his love for her, and, by purchasing the saxophone, encourages her future creativity and intellectual prowess.

Homer is certainly willing to stand up for his children in times of crisis and in the face of danger. These qualities certainly help to portray Homer as a good and decent father. For example, in "Two Bad Neighbors," Homer defends Bart against former President Bush after Bush spanks the boy. In season thirteen, Homer creates the police force Springshield

---

[*] *The Simpsons Archive:* www.snpp.com

mainly because Lisa's Malibu Stacy dolls were stolen from the Simpson home. In many episodes, Homer acts as a decent man and as a thoughtful father.

Homer as the "Bad" Father

Bart, to Homer: We're fighting over who loves you more.
Lisa, pushing Bart: You love him more!
Bart: No, you love him more!

There are also episodes in which Homer is portrayed as a sub-par father. For example, in "Three Men and a Comic Book," Marge tells Homer to check on the boys. Homer looks out the window, sees Bart and his buddies choking each other and says they're fine. In addition, he also encourages fierce competition between Bart and Lisa (certainly not a great idea). For example, in "Lisa on Ice," Homer attends the hockey game that features Bart's team versus Lisa's team. During a crucial point in the game, Homer says: "Oh, my God, Marge. A penalty shot, with only four seconds left. It's your child versus mine! The winner will be showered with praise, the loser will be taunted and booed until my throat is sore."

Another example of Homer's parenting capabilities (or lack thereof) may be found in the episode "Marge Be Not Proud." In the episode, Bart steals from the local Try-N-Save store. Homer attempts to punish him: "I've figured out the boy's punishment. First: he's grounded. No leaving the house, not even for school. Second: no eggnog. In fact, no nog, period. And third, absolutely no stealing for three months." Obviously, this punishment lacks substance and quality. In fact, it is severely flawed. Once again, it is Homer's ignorance that bounds him in situations such as these. Homer does not want Bart to steal ever again, but cannot effectively verbalize this declaration. He might have the right idea, but he's lucky that his children have Marge as their mother.

Perhaps Homer's worst display of parenting may be examined by means of an analysis of the episode entitled "Homer Alone." In the episode, Homer is forced to take responsibility for Maggie, the youngest of the three Simpson children. During Homer's brief stint as the primary caretaker for Maggie, he does the following: "He uses a staple gun to fasten Maggie's diaper. He sits on top of her while watching TV from the couch. He prepares her 9 a.m. feeding at 11:45 a.m."[*] Maggie feels a close, parental bond with Marge and later sets out to look for her. Who could possibly blame her? Homer certainly does not act as the ideal father in this particular episode.

Finally, in "Barting Over," the series' 300th episode, Bart is at odds with Homer because Homer spent all of the money that Bart had earned as a child making Baby Stink Breath commercials. Homer acts selfishly by squandering all of Bart's money, which Marge noted was supposed to be used toward Bart's college fund. Homer's selfish tendencies also serve to prevent him from acting appropriately, and being deemed a good father.

The Forgotten One: Maggie

Maggie, as noted in a later chapter, is the oft-forgotten third child in the Simpson clan. By viewing life through her eyes, we can gain some insight into how she perceives Homer. In one particular episode, she does not care to be identified with being a member of the Simpson family (until Marge comes and she crawls towards her). Homer also asked Maggie to come to him, but she would not do so. In another episode, Homer attempts to teach Maggie how to swim, and

---

[*] *The Simpsons: A Complete Guide to Our Favorite Family*, p. 79

as a test of trust, the instructor tells all of the fathers to catch the babies when they jump into the pool of water. All of the other babies jump into the pool, while Maggie remains on the outside of the pool. She does not trust Homer to save her. However, in the same episode, Maggie saves Homer when he nearly drowns in the ocean. She may not have complete trust in Homer (it is kind of difficult to trust a man of sub-par intelligence), but she certainly possesses a special love for him. As mentioned in the chapter devoted to Maggie, she also saved Homer when mobsters were going to shoot him. In "Lisa's First Word," Maggie uttered her first and only word: "Daddy." By referring to Homer as "Daddy," she demonstrates a special degree of respect for her father, unseen previously as Bart often refers to his father as "Homer." (Interestingly, Lisa was able to pronounce "Bart," "David Hasselhoff," and "Homer," but did not say "Daddy" when she was a baby). In this episode, we get the sense that Maggie may very well be Homer's special little girl. In "And Maggie Makes Three," Homer flashes back to a time when he was unhappy about his job, and explains that Maggie's birth served to cheer him up. Homer tells Lisa that all of Maggie's baby pictures are posted in his office.

Still, there is evidence that serves to contradict the aforementioned viewpoint. For example, Homer has in the past forgotten that Maggie exists. (She is the quiet one, so she is the most likely to be forgotten). In "The Springfield Files" (one of my personal favorite episodes), Homer is drunk in Moe's Tavern and describes his family to F.B.I. agents Mulder and Scully: "… Bart, girl Bart, and the one who doesn't talk. And then there's the fat guy. How I loathe him." Of course, Homer is drunk, but he does mention the defining characteristic of Maggie: quiescence.

Trying to be a good father, in the Blockoland episode

Homer: You can't fight city hall, kids.
Marge: That's a terrible lesson to teach your kids.
Homer: What do you mean? I always tell them that. I told
    them that twice yesterday and again as they were
    going to sleep.

Homer often attempts to be a good father, but falls short
in his efforts. For example, in "Saturdays of Thunder",
Homer wants to learn more about Bart, but doesn't really
know where to begin. He takes the National Fatherhood
Institute Test:

Marge: Name one of your child's friends.
Homer: Uh, let's see, Bart's friends... Well, there's the fat
    kid with the thing...uh, the little wiener who's always
    got his hands in his pockets.
Marge: They want a name, Homer, not a vague descrip-
    tion.
Homer: Okay... Hank.
Marge: Hank? Hank who?
Homer: Hank...Jones.
Marge: Homer, you made that up. Question two, who is
    your son's hero?
Homer: Steve McQueen.
Marge: That's your hero. Name another dad you talk to
    about parenting.
Homer: Next.
Marge: What are your son's hobbies?
Homer: Kids don't have hobbies.
Marge: Oh, really? Well maybe you should go out to the
    garage and see.
*(Homer goes out to the garage and finds Bart hammering away
on his racer.)*

Homer: Bart Bart!

Bart: What?

Homer: You don't have any hobbies, do you boy?

Bart: No, not really.

Homer: Well that's what I—wait a minute, what are you doing?

Bart: Building a soapbox derby racer.

Homer: Oooooh! That's a hobby!

Bart: Hey, so it is.

Homer: Oh, my God! I don't know jack about my boy!

(Homer starts to sob as Marge, Patty, and Selma stand around him.)

Homer: I'm a bad father!

Selma: You're also fat!

Homer: I'm also fat!*

Later in the same episode, Homer attempts to find a way to become a good father. (Homer's plans often center on a quick-fix method or approach.) He visits the National Fatherhood Institute where he speaks with a good father. Homer is given a copy of *Fatherhood* by Bill Cosby. (For a more in-depth discussion centered on *Bill Cosby* versus *The Simpsons*, please see Chapter 9). Here is Homer's conversation with a good father:

Dave: Mr. Simpson, if you want to be a good father, you have to spend time with your son.

Homer: Well, that's easy for you to say, you...preachy...egg-headed...institute guy! How much do you see *your* son?

Dave: Why don't you ask him yourself? Homer, meet Dave, Jr.

Homer: [stunned] Huh?

Dave: How's your research, coming, son?

Dave, Jr: I think we're near a breakthrough.

---

* *The Simpsons: A Complete Guide to Our Favorite Family*, p. 71

Dave: Good work.
Dave, Jr: [leaving] Thanks, Dad.
Homer: Oh, how I envy you.
Dave: Homer, that easy back-and-forth you just wit-
    nessed didn't happen
overnight. It took years of effort.[*]

Certainly, Homer does not like hearing Dave say that
becoming a good father takes years of effort. Still, Homer
attempts to become a good father in this episode, and helps
Bart build his soapbox derby racer.

Homer also begins to read Bill Cosby's book:

Homer: [reading] Cosby's First Law of Intergenerational
    Perversity: No matter what you tell your child to do,
    he will always do the opposite. Huh?
[inner voice] Don't you get it!? You gotta use reverse psychology!
[out loud] Well, that sounds too complicated.
[inner voice] Okay, *don't* use reverse psychology.
[out loud] All right, I will!![†]

In other episodes, Homer realizes his shortcomings as a
father. In "Simpsoncalifragilisticexpiala-D'oh-cious," for
example, Homer sings, "I'd rather drink a beer than win
father of the year." Perhaps this statement sums up Homer's
position on fathering. He may want to be a good father, but,
for the most part, will not work hard for extended periods of
time to achieve this end. At times, Homer overtly displays
great strides toward becoming a good father, but ultimately
falls short of being deemed a good father. He is bound to a
life of laziness and stupidity — barriers which serve to hurt
his chances of becoming a good father.

---

[*] http://www.snpp.com
[†] http://www.snpp.com

Homer's "Quick Fix" Approach to Parenting

In "Saturdays of Thunder," Homer utilizes his "quick fix" approach to life when his parenting techniques are placed in question. As Marge tells him: "Homer, I've always said you were a good father. I've always defended you when people put you down... But I guess I was wrong. You are a bad father."

A few brief moments later, Homer successfully answers the questions on the Fatherhood Quotient exam. He is elated by the fact that he was able to answer the first three questions on the test: "Wow, I'm one question away from being a perfect father." He then decides to fool himself into believing that he truly discusses parenting with another father, specifically Ned Flanders: "I talked to Flanders about parenting – I'm a perfect father!"

Homer then drives down to the soap-box derby racing championship and offers Bart some words of encouragement: "Do it for your old man, boy." After Bart wins the race, Bart caps the scene off: "I was riding alone out there. But someone was with me in spirit. This is for *you*, Dad."

In this scene, Homer and Bart are arguably as close as they have ever been during the course of the series. When Bart is scolded by Marge for being a sore winner after he laughs at Nelson (the loser in the race), Homer supports Bart's insensitive treatment of Nelson. It is here that we realize what message the writers are attempting to purvey to the audience: a good father is loyal to his son at all times. The father/son bond is as significant in Simpsonian life as it is in contemporary American society.

As the episode draws to a close, and we hear a small segment of "Wind Beneath My Wings," we realize that although Homer may not be considered a good father by most standards, he does demonstrate true loyalty to his son. Homer's "quick-fix" approach to parenting was surprisingly successful. Homer is a lucky guy because he is able to truly convince himself that he is a great father.

There are dozens of other *Simpsons* episodes which focus on Homer's role as a father. It is impossible to discuss every example of Homer's role of a father. However, I would recommend the reader visit *The Simpsons* Archive (www.snpp.com) and review some of the following episodes in addition to the episodes already discussed in this chapter:

★ "Lisa's Substitute"

Lisa falls in love with Mr. Bergstrom, the substitute teacher, and is angered by Homer's lack of interest in her interests.

★ "Lisa the Vegetarian"

At first Homer is hesitant to accept Lisa's stance on becoming a vegetarian, but eventually learns to accept his daughter's wishes.

★ "Homer's Phobia"

The episode in which the family (excluding Homer) befriends John, a gay man, whom Homer fears is encouraging homosexual tendencies in Bart. Homer sincerely worries about Bart becoming gay, especially when Bart wears a Hawaiian shirt: "There's only two kinds of guys who wear those shirts—gay guys and big fat party animals. And Bart doesn't look like a big fat party animal."

★ "Bart After Dark"

The episode in which Bart works at the Burlesque house.

★ "Brawl in the Family"

The episode in which the Flanders family adopts the Simpson children because Homer and Marge are deemed bad parents.

★ "The Tell Tale Head"

The episode in which Bart is threatened by an angry mob. Homer stands by his son.

★ "Jaws Wired Shut"

The episode in which Homer can't talk as a result of an injury incurred to his mouth. Homer listens to his family, and takes an interest in the affairs of his wife and children. When Bart opens up to him and discusses the fact that he is deemed a class clown by his classmates—Bart was expected to laugh at the name of the substitute teacher, Mrs. Doody—Homer's brain is at work and silently says: "Wow, Bart has feelings. Hehehehe. Mrs. Doody."

★ "The Parent Rap"

Homer is deemed a bad parent, and Judge Constance Harm (played by Jane Kaczmarek) forces him to be tethered to Bart.

Homer's Parental Guidance

The following quotes are examples of Homer's advice to his children and guidance that he has provided them.

★ "Bart, a woman is like beer. They look good, they smell good, and you'd step over your own mother just to get one!"

★ "Now son, you don't want to drink beer. That's for Daddies, and kids with fake IDs."

★ "Marge, don't discourage the boy! Weaseling out of things is important to learn. It's what separates us from the animals...except the weasel."

★ "If you really want something in life you have to work for it. Now quiet, they're about to announce the lottery numbers."

★ "Son, when you participate in sporting events, it's not whether you win or lose: it's how drunk you get."

★ "The code of the schoolyard, Marge! The rules that teach a boy to be a man. Let's see. Don't tattle. Always make fun of those different from you. Never say anything, unless you're sure everyone feels exactly the same way you do. What else…"

★ "Quiet, you kids. If I hear one more word, Bart doesn't get to watch cartoons, and Lisa doesn't get to go to college."

★ Bart: I'm through with working. Working is for chumps.
   Homer: Son, I'm proud of you. I was twice your age
      before I figured that out.

★ "Kids are great, Apu. You can teach them to hate the things you hate and they practically raise themselves now-a-days, you know, with the internet and all."

★ Bart: Gee… Sorry for being born.
   Homer: I've been waiting for so long to hear that.

★ "I want to share something with you — the three sentences that will get you through life. Number one: 'Cover for me.' Number two: 'Oh, good idea, boss.' Number three: 'It was like that when I got here.'"

★ "I will live to be 42. Oh, only 42 ?!? I won't even live to see my children die."

★ Homer: Hey boy! Wanna play catch?
   Bart: No thanks, dad.
   Homer: When a son doesn't want to play catch with his
      father something is definitely wrong.
   Grandpa: I'll play catch with you!
   Homer: Go home.

★   Homer: Kids, kids! I'm not gonna die! That only happens to bad people!
Bart: What about Abraham Lincoln?
Homer: Err... He sold poisoned milk to school children.
Marge: Homer!
Homer: Hey, I'm just trying to make it easier on them.

Homer's Love for His Children

He may not be the ideal father, but he does love his children. In "One Fish, Two Fish..." Homer is told that he is going to die (he had eaten sushi that was believed to be poisoned). He says goodbye to his three children:

"Goodbye Maggie: Stay as sweet as you are.
Goodbye Lisa: I know you'll make me proud.
Goodbye Bart: [long pause] I like your sheets."

In "Homer's Triple Bypass," Marge allows Bart and Lisa to enter the operating room.

Homer: Kids, I wanna give you some words to remember me by, if something happens. Let's see...er... Oh, I'm no good at this.
Lisa: [Whispers into Homer's ear.]
Homer: Bart, the saddest thing about this is I'm not going to see you grow up...
Lisa: [Whispers into Homer's ear.]
Homer: ...because I know you're gonna turn out well, with or without your old man.
Bart: Thanks, Dad.
Homer: And Lisa...
Bart: [whispers into Homer's ear]
Homer: I guess this is the time to tell you...

Bart: [whispers into Homer's ear]
Homer: ...that you're adopted and I don't like you. [Real-
    izes.] Bart!
Bart: [whispers into Homer's ear]
Homer: But don't worry, because you've got a big brother
    who loves you and will always look out for you.
Lisa: Oh, Dad. [Hugs him.]
    -- *possibly Homer's final words ("Homer's Triple Bypass")*

As critic Jeff MacGregor pointedly notes, "It is Homer
Simpson who drives the show." As a moving, ever expand-
ing satire, he is at once the best and worst of American dad-
ness. He is forever wanting the things he'll never have,
scheming to get them and failing, his appetites and disap-
pointments as classic as the central conflicts from which all
great theater and literature derives."*

In the words of Homer Simpson, "That's the end of that
chapter."

---

* MacGregor, Jeff. *More Than Sight Gags and Subversive Satire*. New
York *Times*, 20 June 1999: Television/Radio 27.

CHAPTER 2

Bart: America's Bad Boy?

"I didn't do it. Nobody saw me do it. You can't prove anything."

— Bart Simpson

"Even I wouldn't do that, and I'm America's bad boy."

— Bart Simpson

Prank calls. A slingshot. Disrespect. These are all unmistakable trademarks of the character of Bart Simpson. But is Bart really *that* bad? Or is the 10-year-old Simpson boy simply crying out for attention? In this section, I will answer the aforementioned questions, while also analyzing Bart's influence on children in contemporary society.

In the earlier episodes of *The Simpsons*, the writers of the series introduced the American public to the bad boy antics of Bartholomew Simpson. The writers realized that bad was funny — for a while, anyway. After several seasons passed by, however, the writers made a fundamental change in the direction of the series: Homer became dumber, and subsequently funnier, while Bart's bad behavior toned down a few notches. Homer eventually became the lead star of the series. The writers came to the correct conclusion that "dumb" is consistently funnier than "bad." In fact, if the writers had not made this significant change in the direction of the series, *The Simpsons* would probably not have enjoyed such a long, successful run. There are only so many prank calls that Bart could have made before Simpsons fans would have had enough of him.

Bart's irreverence for all authoritative figures in early episodes of *The Simpsons* is overtly obvious, even to the casual Simpsons fan. During the early 1990's, Fox sold many licensing contracts to companies who were looking to cash in on "Simpson Mania," which was simply a corollary of "Bart Mania." For example, t-shirts possessed the potential for harm. Back in the early 1990's, everyone wanted to be like Bart. Still, the t-shirts, contrary to popular opinion at the time, did not serve as a harbinger for disaster. Young school children did not run amok with slingshots. Prank calls may have become more popular in our society, but, for the most part, people did not have to change their phone numbers because of this phenomenon. And, perhaps most importantly, children still called their fathers "dad," as opposed to referring to them by their first name (as Bart did in early episodes).

So why didn't Bart's antics create serious troubles in contemporary society (as conservatives predicted they would)? The reason that Bart's bad behavior did not influence the behavior of young children is that *The Simpsons* was (and still is) aimed at a vastly different audience: adults. This certainly helps to explain why *The Simpsons* airs during prime-time (when adults can watch) as opposed to during the daytime (along with other children's shows). Adults found the humor in Bart's antics, while young children, even if exposed to the show, didn't really understand most aspects of the series. Sure, children might have seen Bart make a prank call or two, but they would not have grasped the meaning behind most of the episodes. Thus, the influence of *The Simpsons* was — and is — greater on adults than on children.

This point brings us back to my initial thesis: *The Simpsons* is more than just a cartoon. Cartoons are created for children;

The Simpsons was intended for adults. Case and point: what child would understand the political satire of Mayor Quimby or the stereotypical portrayal of police (Chief Wiggum)? Children take Simpson characters for what they are, not what they represent. Bart represents the American bad boy. He is a reflection of children in society, and does not add fuel to the fire pertaining to the misbehavior of American kids. Children made prank phone calls long before Bart did, and shot rocks out of slingshots prior to the Dennis the Menace era.

Thus, Bart was bad, but his mischievousness did not have much of a negative impact on American children. Although some children did watch *The Simpsons*, they probably were able to understand that Bart was a bad boy. To slightly alter my earlier contention that held that everyone wanted to be like Bart, children wanted to be like Bart—but only at specific times. Bart was cool when he misbehaved, but American children would quickly learn that performing Bart's antics would land them in serious trouble. Even the early episodes of *The Simpsons* emphasized this point: Homer choking Bart, while a humorous scene, is certainly not a pleasant one.

Bart is rarely rewarded for his misdeeds. Consider the scene before each episode in which Bart writes on the chalkboard as punishment for his actions. Viewers are clearly able to see that there are consequences for behaving badly. In one particular episode, for example, Bart steals a video game from the local Try-N-Save store. When he is caught, he loses the trust of his entire family. Similarly, when Bart shoots and kills a bird (albeit accidentally), he temporarily loses the respect of his mother.

There have been numerous other times when Bart was punished for misbehaving. For example, Homer once decreed that Bart not be allowed to see *Itchy and Scratchy: The Movie*. The fact that Bart was punished for his misdeeds in this episode enables him to grow up as a successful individual later in life. (At the end of the episode, the writers take the viewing audience into the future, and we are able to see that because Bart was punished while he was young, he was able to grow up into a mature, well-functioning adult).

Another example of Bart being punished for his misbehavior may be examined in the episode entitled "Radio Bart." In the episode, Bart was punished for duping the townspeople into believing that a boy (Timmy O'Toole) had fallen down a well. However, poetic justice was served when Bart himself fell down the well, and the townspeople, who had been so sympathetic to the imaginary Timmy O'Toole's dilemma, were reluctant to save Bart. Bart, of course, was eventually rescued, but the fear that he felt while stuck in the bottom of the well served to teach him a valuable lesson: lying can get you into trouble.

Now that we've concluded that Bart doesn't have too much of a negative influence on children, let's review some of the times that Bart has misbehaved. Please note that the following plot situations and quotes were taken from episodes that aired during seasons 1 and 2.

Disrepect toward Homer

★ Homer: Don't worry, son. You don't have to follow in my footsteps.
Bart: I don't even like to use the bathroom after you.

★ In "There's No Disgrace Like Home":

Mr. Burns: And make yourself at home.
Bart: Hear that, Dad? You can lie around in your underwear and scratch yourself.

From the same episode, after Burns sees a father kiss his son:

Burns: Awww. That's the kind of family unity I like
    see. Smithers, get that man's name. I predict big things
    for him down at the power plant.
Homer: Quick, Bart, give me a kiss.
Bart: Kiss you? But, Dad, I'm your kid!
Homer: Bart, please. Five bucks for a kiss.

Bart's Bad Behavior

★ In "Homer's Night Out," Bart uses his spy camera to take
a picture of Homer dancing with Princess Kashmir.

★ In "Bart the Daredevil," Bart disobeys Homer and leaves
to jump the gorge. (Homer does eventually prevent him from
doing so, however.)

★ In the Tracy Ullman Show short entitled "Bart's Night-
mare," Bart eats too many cookies, and has a bad dream
where Homer catches him and threatens to punish him.

★ In "Bart the Genius," Bart switches tests with Martin
Prince.

★ In "Simpson and Delilah," Bart breaks Homer's bottle of
Dimoxinil.

★ In "Bart Gets an F," Bart squirts ketchup on Martin's butt
and says, "Little ketchup for your buns, papa?"

★ In "Two Cars in Every Garage and Three Eyes on Every
Fish," Bart says, "Dear God, we paid for all this stuff
ourselves, so thanks for nothing."

★ In "Homer vs. Lisa and the Eighth Commandment," he
says, "Man, I wish I was an adult so I could break the rules."
(In this episode, Bart also says "hell" many times.)

★ In "Bart the General"

O   33   /'s *Marching Song Lyrics:*
arithmetic
..... got an A, but I was sick
In English class I did the best
because I cheated on the test

★ In "Dead Putting Society," at the library:

Lisa (loading Bart with books): And, finally, the most important book of all, the *Tao Te Ching* by Lao Tzu.
Bart: Lisa, we can't afford all these books.
Lisa: Bart, we're just going to borrow them.
Bart: (winks slyly) Oh, heh, heh. Gotcha.

★ In "Bart's Dog Gets an F":
Lisa: Get my homework from Miss Hoover.
Bart: Homework? Lisa, you wasted chicken pox! Don't
  waste the mumps!

Why Bart's Not Like He Used To Be

Crazy Old Man (singing): He ain't what he used to be...
(Note that I replaced "she" with "he")

"If I can use an old phrase—'Ay Carumba!'"
— *Bart, in a season 14 episode*

Bart just isn't the same anymore. He's somewhat softer spoken, and generally quieter. He's not as rude anymore either. (In fact, in recent seasons Bart has most often referred to Homer as "dad"). Thus, it seems as though society has had an impact on Bart. For example, the nation-wide condemnation of the Columbine high school shootings gave "bad" a new name. Bart would never perform such an evil act, and if prompted, would probably realize that his petty rock slinging and parental disrespect pale in comparison with the actions of several other adolescents. In fact, Bart's actions may be deemed innocuous when compared with such acts of evil. Thus, Bart can no longer define what "bad" is. People in contemporary society have already outlined their definition of "bad," and somehow, Bart doesn't fit their definition. Bart is basically a good kid, and when he does do something wrong, he feels badly about it. In this way, he hasn't changed much at all.

I've already theorized that Bart has changed as a result of society, but what specifically has changed about Bart? Four words: he has toned down. Bart still has his occasional lapses: for example, he angered Homer with his creation of the 'Angry Dad' internet cartoon. Still, these instances are rarer than they were in previous seasons. Bart is by no means the ideal child, but his bad behavior is no longer the central focus of the series. In fact, fewer episodes in recent seasons are centered on any aspect of Bart's character. He's still a member of the "fabulous five," i.e., the Simpson clan, but he has handed the spotlight to Homer. Perhaps that's why the series' 300th episode ("Barting Over") was so interesting.

The episode focused on Bart's understandable anger at Homer. (Homer spent the money that Bart earned doing "Baby Stink Breath" commercials when he was a baby). The episode centered on three main subjects: Bart, Homer, and skateboarding. Interestingly, this was one of the few episodes in which Bart became *really* angry at Homer. By contrast, in other episodes Bart performed actions that were against Homer's wishes, and had to defend himself by denying responsibility. As Bart memorably noted in "Moaning Lisa": "I didn't do it. No one saw me do it. No one can prove anything." In the 300th episode, however, Homer was on the defensive end. It was almost as though the roles of Homer and Bart had been *reversed*. Homer acted childishly: he initially attempted not to reveal to Bart how upset he was after Bart moved out of the house. Bart, on the other hand, acted independently: he moved out into his own loft. In these ways, the writers of *The Simpsons* demonstrated their unique ability to reverse the roles of some of the central figures on the series.

The aforementioned episode is important to consider because it is one of the few episodes aired during the last couple of seasons that centered on Bart. Bart seemed more mature in this episode—until he became scared of sleeping alone in his new loft. It was then that we realize that Bart hasn't changed much at all: he's still a ten-year-old boy, a "bratty brother," and an incorrigible son. When Bart initially would not obey his parents and return home, however, something interesting happened: his family missed him. Lisa was stuck with the Indian burn in the shape of a heart that Bart had put on her arm. Homer was in tears (though he initially hid this from Bart), and Marge was struck with grief over Bart's sudden departure. If Maggie could speak, she probably would have called out for Bart as well. So if Bart is truly America's "bad boy," why isn't his family *happy* that he's gone? The answer is quite simple: Bart is not America's bad boy. He's just your everyday, run of the mill ten-year-old. And his family loves him: Lisa's first word was "Bart." Marge has called Bart her "special little guy." Homer and Bart have, on at least a few occasions, said that they love each other.

Bush vs. Bart a la Dennis the Menace

"A slingshot in his back pocket?! Who does he think he is—Dennis the Menace?"

—Erin

"Two Bad Neighbors" was a monumental episode in the long run of *The Simpsons*. In the episode, Bart got on the nerves of former President George Bush. Bart's antics were similar to those of Dennis the Menace: for example, Bart accidentally destroyed Bush's memoirs. However, Bart also demonstrated why some critics blame Bart for the tendency of American children to disrespect adults. For example, take the following quote from this episode:

> George Bush: In my day children didn't call their elders by their first name.
> Bart: Well, welcome to the 20th century, George.

Later in the episode, we sympathize with Bart after Bush spanks him. Simpsonian politics are prevalent at this point: the classic conservative (Bush) is seen spanking a helpless young boy, while the Simpson family (whose members are more liberal than Bush) is outraged by Bush's actions. Bart behaves particularly badly in this episode, but liberal Americans would undoubtedly have qualms with Bush's punishment of the boy.

Is Bart Happy Being Bart?

In a Season 13 episode, Bart explains his frustrations to Homer. Bart speaks about being the class clown, and notes that it sickens him. This is one of the rare instances in which we are allowed entrance into the mind of Bart. Bart evidently wants to be perceived as a good child—at least in this episode. But his fate has been forever sealed: when there are T-shirts of Bart saying "I'm Bart Simpson / Who the hell are you?" people tend to think about him in a certain way. He may have matured somewhat in recent seasons, but first impressions mean everything.

I've already discussed whether or not Bart is actually a bad seed, but the question remains of whether Bart is happy being *perceived* as America's bad boy. The answer to this question is two-fold: at times, Bart seems to enjoy the attention that he receives as a direct result of his bad behavior. On the other hand, the aforementioned example of Bart's frustration pertaining to being deemed the "class clown" serves to contradict this point. So it comes down to this: Bart enjoys being perceived as America's bad boy when it brings him glory. At other times, however, Bart wants to fit in, and desperately wants to be like his peers. It's almost as if Bart, over the years, has become tired of being "bad." Still, he is only ten years old, and does have occasional lapses in character. So the next time Bart does something that authority figures would not approve of, do the boy one favor: Don't have a cow, man.*

More Bart Quotes

★ "I only lied because it was the easiest way for me to get what I wanted."

★ In "Lisa's Sax," Bart's makes fun of Principal Skinner:

Bart (singing): Skinner is a nut / He has a rubber butt!
Skinner: Young man, I can assure you my posterior is nothing more than flesh, bone, and that metal plate I got in 'Nam. Now I want to knock off that potty talk right now.
Bart: The principal said potty!
Skinner: You listen to me, son. You've just started school, and the path you choose now may be the one you follow for the rest of your life. Now what do you say?
Bart: Eat my shorts.

---

* One important episode to consider in which Bart acts immorally is entitled "Miracle on Evergreen Terrace." In the episode, Bart accidentally burns the family's Christmas presents. He then lies and says that a burglar stole the gifts. Authority figures certainly would not have approved of Bart's actions in the first half of this episode.

★ Also in "Lisa's Sax":

Teacher (reading): ...and the ugly duckling was amazed to realize it had grown into a beautiful swan. So you see children, there is hope for everyone.
Young Bart: Even me?
Teacher: No.

★ Excerpt from "Do the Bartman":

Bart: Hey, what's happenin' dude?
I'm a guy with a rep for bein' rude.
Terrorizin' people wherever I go
It's not intentional, just keepin' the flow.
Fixin' test scores to get the best scores...
Droppin' banana peels all over the floor,
I'm the kid that made delinquency an art.
Last name Simpson; first name, Bart.

★ From "Miracle on Evergreen Terrace":

(Bart kneels at hid bedside in his pajamas, hands pressed together, as if in prayer.)
Bart: Dear Santa, if you bring me lots of good stuff, I promise not to do anything bad between now and when I wake up. (When Bart opens his arms, he hits his elbow on his nightstand.)
Bart: Ow! I'll kill you! (Bart lunges for his nightstand to smash it.)

Some of Bart's Prank Phone Calls

★ "Phone call for Al...Al Coholic...is there an Al Coholic here?"

★ "Oliver Clothesoff! Call for Oliver Clothesoff!"

.. "Uh, is I.P. Freely here? Hey everybody, I.P. Freely!"

★ "Hey is there a Butz here? Semour Butz! Hey everyone, I wanna Semour Butz!"

★ "Uh, Homer Sexual? Aw, come on, come on one of you guys gotta be Homer Sexual!"

.. "Mike Rotch! Mike Rotch! Hey, has anyone seen Mike Rotch?"

.. "Bea O'Problem! Come on guys do I have a Bea O'Problem!"

.. "Uh, Jacques Strap! Hey guys, I'm looking for a Jacques Strap!"

★ "Ivana Tinkle! Ivana Tinkle! All right guys, put down your glasses. Ivana Tinkle!!"

.. "Amanda Huginkiss. Is there Amanda Huginkiss here? Why can't I find Amanda Huginkiss?!"

.. "Uh, Hugh Jass? Oh, someone check the men's room for a Hugh Jass!"

.. "Can I speak to a Mrs. Booger? First name Alita."

CHAPTER 3

Marge: Holding the Family Together

"I sense greatness in my family, too—it's not a greatness that others can see, but it's there. And if it's not, then we're at least average."
— *Marge Simpson ["There's No Disgrace Like Home"]*

In contemporary society, the mother generally takes much of the responsibility in taking care of the family. Mothers know what's best for their families. In the Simpson household, Marge is the character that takes care of her family. Just as an egg holds a cake together, Marge holds her family together.

Marge's crucial role as the unofficial caretaker of the Simpson family was made evident in the episode in which Marge breaks her leg and must go to the hospital ("Little Big Mom"). In the episode, Marge asks Lisa to tend to the needs of Homer, Bart, and Maggie. Of course, Lisa runs into problems: when Bart and Homer decide to play Marco Polo in the house and flood the entire kitchen. Additionally, neither Bart nor Homer was eager to do the chores Lisa attempted to assign to them. Marge is sorely missed by everyone in the family. Even though Homer and Bart had more "freedom" under Lisa's reign as caretaker, they undoubtedly would have welcomed Marge's guidance and orders. In the episode, we learn that Bart and Homer cannot take proper care of themselves. For example, when Homer came into the kitchen wearing only his underwear, Lisa questioned him:

Homer: Morning.
Lisa: Dad! Where are your clothes?
Homer: I don't know.
Lisa: Don't tell me Mom dresses you.
Homer: I guess. Or one of her friends.

Lisa is more intelligent than Marge, but because she is a young girl she lacks Marge's motherly instincts. Marge's role is important because she ensures that everything runs smoothly in the household. The examples from this particular episode serve as evidence of her importance in the everyday affairs of the Simpson family.

The aforementioned episode is an important one to consider when defining the role of Marge. Her importance is only fully realized when she is gone. The situation outlined in this episode is similar to those that arise when a family member leaves home for an extended period of time in modern society. Like other contemporary mothers, Marge is taken for granted. She works assiduously to render specific services for each member of her family, but she is never truly appreciated until she leaves. It is when she leaves that the family (especially Lisa) truly begins to appreciate her value to the well being of the entire family.

Marge is also taken advantage of at certain times. For example, in the Shary Bobbins episode, Marge begins to lose her hair and visits Dr. Hibbert. While at the hospital, she receives a phone call from Bart and Lisa.

Bart: I want a glass of milk.
Lisa: Me, too.

Dr. Hibbert informs Marge that she is suffering from stress, and given the aforementioned example, it is obvious that Marge is often take advantage of. It is a wonder to marvel at how she keeps the Simpson family together, given their lack of independence.

Marge's Hair

It's blue and many, many, many inches long. You can hide your family's savings in it. At its fullest, it can even support a beach umbrella. But what does Marge's hair say about women in general?

For centuries, women have taken great pride in their hairstyles. By drawing Marge with an eccentric hairstyle, the animators of *The Simpsons* have seemingly mocked women's obsession with their hair. Details such as this one are what make *The Simpsons* a truly unique public phenomenon. To some viewers, Marge's hair is a simple joke; to others it mocks women's' age-old obsession with their hair.

Married With Children similarly mocked women's obsession with their hair. Peg Bundy had a far from conventional hairdo on the series. True comedy, at its best, mocks real aspects of our everyday lives. Both *The Simpsons* and *Married With Children* are successful because they examine reality, and satirize its everyday elements. (For a more detailed discussion of the role of Marge and other TV wives, see Chapter 9.)

CHAPTER 4

Lisa: True Simpson or Potential Future College Student?

"Dad, as intelligence goes up, happiness often goes down. In fact, I made a graph. I make a lot of graphs."
— *Lisa, in "Homr"*

"Lisa, I'm taking the coward's way out. But before I do, I just want you to know: Being smart made me appreciate how amazing you really are."
— *Homer, after becoming smart in the same episode*

"Trust in yourself and you can achieve anything."
— *Lisa (via the Lisa the Lionheart talking doll), in "Lisa vs. Malibu Stacy"*

The Simpson family is comprised of five unique individuals. If we were to group the family members into separate spheres, we would almost certainly place Homer, Marge, Bart, and Maggie together, and place Lisa in her own separate (and special) group.

Why all the fuss over Lisa?

Lisa Simpson is a unique character who differs in many ways from the rest of her family. She is remarkably bright (a proud member of MENSA), a left-wing activist, and is rarely deterred from speaking her mind (she has appeared numerous times on Kent Brockman's "Smartline"). Lisa is extremely motivated to do well in life, which conflicts with Homer's principle that "trying is the first step towards failure." She is in a class of her own as she resides in a "town of lowbrows, nobrows, and ignorami." As Lisa notes, "[Springfield] has eight malls, but no symphony. Thirty-two bars but no alternative theater. Thirteen stores that begin with 'Le Sex'." Lisa is obviously dissatisfied with the insipid nature of Springfield's residents, and would love to experience "true" culture.

Lisa demonstrates her exuberance, as well as her keen ambition, in the episode entitled "Lisa vs. Malibu Stacy." In the episode, Lisa challenges the manufacturers of the Malibu Stacy doll (a Barbie-like doll) to portray females as intelligent and not mere sex objects. In an important statement, Lisa notes, "I've got a solution—you and I are going to make our own talking doll. She'll have the wisdom of Gertrude Stein and the wit of Cathy Guisewite, the tenacity of Nina Totenberg and the common sense of Elizabeth Cady Stanton. And to top it off, the down-to-earth good looks of Eleanor Roosevelt."

Lisa feels very strongly about women's rights. This marks a fundamental difference between Lisa and other women residing in Springfield. Case and point: Springfield male executive (Wolf) to female employee (Harper) whistles and audaciously exclaims: "Hey, Jiggles! Grab a pad and back that gorgeous butt in here." Harper (coyly): "Oh, you, get away…" (girlish giggles). Lisa sees the need for change in her society, and is willing to take on the responsibility of spearheading the creation of a new doll that promises to portray women in a more positive and meaningful manner.

If we are to examine Lisa's place in the Simpson family, it behooves us to explore the episode entitled "Lisa the Simpson." In the episode, Lisa fears that since she was born a Simpson, she will become dumber as she grows older. She expresses her fear by sarcastically asking, "Isn't there any way I can change my DNA, like sitting on the microwave?" Lisa is well aware that she is too intelligent to be called a Simpson. However, her Simpsonian roots come to surface, when, after solving a brainteaser in the same episode, she declares, "I got it! Woo-hoo! I mean, 'Splendid'." By saying Homer's classic "woo-hoo" catch phrase, Lisa displays a side of herself to which the audience is exposed on a less consistent basis. Lisa may not be content with being deemed a Simpson, but she is at times unable to escape her background.

In exploring the "Simpson side" of Lisa, it is vital to note her relationship with television. She enjoys watching the cartoon series entitled "The Happy Little Elves," which centers on mindless characters singing and dancing. It would seem that the cartoon would be hardly entertaining for someone with Lisa's academic prowess. Still, Lisa genuinely enjoys watching the cartoon. It is in this example that we begin to realize who Lisa Simpson truly is: an eight-year-old girl who is being raised in a community virtually entirely composed of people with below average intelligence (some notable exceptions include Mr. Burns, Dr. Hibbert, Apu, and Professor Frink). Still, Springfield has been the town with the lowest voter turnout in the presidential election (as stated in "Two Bad Neighbors"). Lisa's family and community have influenced and molded some of her interests. For example, she has learned to love the violent cartoon "Itchy and Scratchy" as a result of spending so much time with Bart.

The aforementioned points serve to portray Lisa as an "average" eight-year-old Simpson child. However, a wealth of wisdom lurks in her witty remarks and commentaries pertaining to Springfield. For instance, after landing a job on a children-run news program, she states "...and I'll be able to tackle all the hard-hitting children news the grown-up controlled media won't touch." In another episode in which the teachers of Springfield Elementary School go on strike, Lisa is nervous about her lack of learning caused by the missed days of school. She frantically remarks "Relax? I can't relax. Nor can I yield, relent, or...only two synonyms? Oh my god!

I'm losing my perspicacity!" (Say "D'oh" if you don't know the definition of perspicacity!) Lisa may be only eight years old, but she's smarter than a lot of her elders.

Obviously, the writers of *The Simpsons* have portrayed Lisa in two strikingly different, perhaps even contradictory, manners. On the one hand, Lisa is an eight-year-old little girl fighting to keep her head above water in a pool comprised of town idiots. On the other hand, she is a political advocate, a vegetarian, an avid reader of *Junior Skeptic* magazine, and as mentioned earlier, a member of the academic institution MENSA. Whatever conclusion we may reach about Lisa, one fact is undeniable: she is a special character. And, if animation technology improves, and the Simpson family is re-invented into real-life, we may see Lisa roaming a college campus. She seems to be headed in this direction.

CHAPTER 5

To Speak or Not to Speak: Maggie Simpson vs. Stewie Griffin

"Those who know don't talk. Those who talk don't know."

— *Tao Te Ching*[*]

"The limits of my language mean the limits of my world."

— *Ludwig Wittgenstein*[†]

In contemporary society, it seems as though people who succeed in life are invariably the same people who speak their minds. Whether or not these people can contribute some worthy ideas to society is debatable. Still, more often than not, the mere expression of one's ideas leads to discussion of those ideas amongst one's peers. In order to explore the aforementioned thoughts in greater detail, it behooves us to enter the world of the people who can have an impact on the future of the world. Perhaps another book may focus on the ideas of important national and international leaders. However, I am going to utilize a somewhat different approach in

[*] Irwin, William. The *Simpsons and Philosophy: The D'oh! Of Homer*. Illinois: Carus Publishing Co., 2001.
[†] *Ibid*.

outlining this particular discourse: let's explore the realm of the *future* leaders of the world — that of cartoon babies!

While college students may feel as though they are members of an influential age group, the fact of the matter is that we are merely the predecessors of future generations. At one point or another, we will pass the torch on to future generations. Thus, it is vital for us to understand the (quiet) world of babies such as Maggie Simpson as well as the (loud) world of Stewie Griffin (from *Family Guy*).

"Speak softly and carry a big stick."

— *Teddy Roosevelt*

"Hear much but maintain silence."

— *Confucius*

Maggie Simpson is an immensely important character for several reasons. Firstly, her character, for the most part, encompasses the virtue of true innocence. For example, Maggie was not sent to prison after accidentally shooting Mr. Burns ("Who Shot Mr. Burns?"). Her actions were certainly far from virtuous, but she was not punished because she did not possess malicious motives for firing the gun. Instead, Maggie is most often viewed as innocuous: her presence in the Springfield community is largely non-detrimental to the town as a whole. Since she is a baby, her actions can never truly be deemed reprehensible, as her very being is composed of a dearth of malevolence.

Still, the soft-spoken Maggie (her only spoken word thus far has been "Daddy") is somewhat intelligent. For example, she saved Homer's life on at least two separate occasions: she fired guns at mobsters and saved Homer when he was drowning in the ocean. In addition, she also played Tchaikovsky's "Dance of the Sugar Plum Fairies" on her toy xylophone.

Maggie is content with her role as the often-forgotten third child (Homer has literally forgotten that she exists on several occasions). Maggie is a likeable baby—and this is not solely a result of her cuteness. For example, when Maggie encountered grizzly bears in an early episode of *The Simpsons*, she is able to win the love, adulation, and most importantly, respect of the fierce bears. Without speaking a single word, she was able to command the bears to bring her another pacifier along with many new toys, which the bears stole from another baby.

Maggie Simpson's soft-spoken demeanor is only viable because she spends virtually all of her time sucking a pacifier. Still, as examined through the aforementioned evidence, Maggie, by means of her "pacifier sucking" can, at times, speak volumes without pronouncing a single word.

Maggie's only significant movement away from the virtue of true innocence lies in her relationship with Gerald, the baby with one eyebrow. When Maggie encounters Gerald, they momentarily stare menacingly into each other's eyes. Of course, the fact that Maggie has an enemy will help her adapt to the adult world. (I'm certain that if President Bush had encountered Clinton when they were babies, they would have exchanged some vicious glances with one another as well.)

Express Yourself

And now we move into the obnoxious world of Stewie Griffin (the talking baby on *Family Guy*). Stewie, who was born holding a map of the world, is seldom hesitant to share his thoughts or add satirical comments in any given episode of *Family Guy*. His unfounded suspicion of the world around him demonstrates a fundamental difference between himself and Maggie Simpson. While Maggie accepts life, Stewie is constantly devising schemes to thwart (what he believes are) attempts by adults to limit his role in the world. Maggie refrains from involving herself in adult situations. While Stewie falls in love with a fellow toddler, namely Janet ("Dammit, Janet"), Maggie does not expose herself to situations in which heartbreak may result. By falling in love, talking back to his parents, and plotting to take over the world, Stewie distances himself from the ideal of true innocence that babies generally possess. Stewie is often more bitter than Maggie because he sets goals for himself that are virtually impossible to accomplish. His wisecracks at the expense of others demonstrate maturity beyond his years: it is precisely this precocious mind-frame that leads to his state of unhappiness.

The question of whether it is better for us to openly express ourselves or remain silent in given situations is open-ended and subject to intense debate. In examining the world of cartoon babies, we come to the conclusion that babies can have an influence on the world. As Maggie teaches us, it is often better to listen and learn from others than to voice our opinions about subjects in which we only possess superficial knowledge. In other words, edification can result if we simply sit back and quietly watch the world around us.

CHAPTER 6

C. Montgomery Burns and the Pursuit of True Happiness

"One dollar for eternal happiness? I'd be happier with the dollar."

— *Mr. Burns*

Homer: Ya know, Mr. Burns, you're the richest guy I know — way richer than Lenny.
Mr. Burns: Yes, but I'd trade it all for a little more.

Mr. Burns holds several distinctions in the city of Springfield. For instance, he is the city's oldest resident, the richest, the most sinister, as well as the most ruthless capitalist. Still, the question of whether C. Montgomery Burns is truly happy is a difficult question to consider. On the one hand, he can afford any luxury he desires, and is given much respect by his loyal confidant, Waylon Smithers. However, there are several instances in which Mr. Burns displays his desire to attain something more out of life. Indeed, there are several distinct times in which Burns exhibits true human emotion — emotions that cannot be satisfactorily abated through the utilization of his plentiful monies.

Mr. Burns' search for true love often crops up in various episodes of *The Simpsons*. For example, Burns dreams about

Marge Simpson flying through his window while he is neatly tucked under his blanket. At this moment, Burns is so entranced by Marge's beauty that suddenly he appears like the rest of us. He is victim to the insuperable conquering power of love—his money cannot buy him Marge's heart. We empathize with Burns, who suddenly appears frail and perhaps innocent in the depths of unrequited love. In this particular situation, the riches that Burns has accumulated are rendered meaningless. Burns' unrequited love for Marge demonstrates that money cannot buy true love—or even happiness.*

In addition to Burns' desire to find true love, we also see the 104-year-old incessantly search for more money in attempts to increase his already prodigious worth. For example, he breaks into the Simpson household and steals the key to the Flying Hellfish treasure. Indeed, Burns demonstrates the characteristics of the ruthless capitalist, who will by no means stop in his quest for profits. However, one may consider why the fragile, 104-year-old Burns would go to such lengths in order to obtain a strictly financial reward. Certainly, one may argue, Burns has all the money he needs, and should have no legitimate reason for risking injury in an attempt to procure such superfluous funds.

Burns's insatiability is psychological, rather than physiological in nature. For example, at his Thanksgiving table, Burns is presented with a huge spread of different foods that Smithers has prepared for him. Burns compliments Smithers on the display, takes one small bite of turkey, and says something to the effect of, "Oh I couldn't possibly eat another bite." Burns may certainly not be considered a glutton, but he does not order Smithers to prepare a smaller meal next year.

---

* Indeed, the middle-class industrialized employee, Homer J. Simpson, is viewed as the fortunate man in this situation, as he has successfully won the heart of Marge. For a more thorough discussion of Homer's role as the industrialized employee, please see a later chapter in this volume.

Despite the fact that Burns does not touch over 99% of the food displayed on the table, the viewer can detect a sense of happiness from Burns as he looks over the tremendous amount of food on the table. Burns is satisfied that the food is available to him, and this is where his insatiability ceases to exist. Once Burns knows that the food is available to him, he dismisses most of it. For him, simply knowing that the food is available is all the satisfaction that he requires.

Similarly, Burns would love to acquire as much money as he possibly can just so he can flaunt it about—he will never be able to spend all of his money. Thus, his feud with Grampa is psychologically based. He does not require the money to build a "safety net," nor does he need any additional monies to finance any luxurious ventures. The only reason that Burns wants to obtain the money is so that he can attain (the impossible goal of) complete and total satiation.

Another important example of Burns's lack of complete happiness may be found through an analysis of his association with his bear, Bobo. Burns's love for his teddy bear is so strong that he is willing to pay a large sum of money to the Simpson family for its return to his hands. Burns teaches us that certain items may be deemed priceless, and that money cannot serve as an adequate substitute for emotional attachment. Although the audience may find it comical that a rich individual holds an emotional attachment to a stuffed animal, we can also relate to the feelings over which Burns has no control. For example, those who have held onto a particular toy or memento for years have experienced similar emotions. C. Montgomery Burns demonstrates that he is no different from the rest of us, despite his vast wealth. At times it seems as though the little things in life, the niceties, so to speak, are what make us truly happy.

Any thorough analysis of Mr. Burns's state of happiness must include a consideration of whether or not Burns is a perfectionist. Let us begin with an analysis of Burns's utilization of the word "excellent" on many occasions. When something goes exactly Burns's way, he taps his fingers together, and utters "excellent." He does so in an almost victorious fashion. His utterance of the word "excellent" demonstrates that Burns becomes content when something is absolutely perfect. Viewers can almost see the joy in stingy old Mr. Burns' eyes when something goes his way.

Perhaps perfectionism is a quality that is essential for a person to gain massive wealth. Mr. Burns will not settle for anything less than perfection in any endeavor. Perhaps this is why his "yes-men" accountants tell him that his stock options are great when they're all but bankrupt. They certainly do not want to report any news to Burns that fails to meet his standard of excellence. If Burns truly is a perfectionist (and the evidence tends to point in this very direction), then it is understandable why he is often unhappy. Life, even for those who are rich, is not always perfect, and perfectionists lack the capability to accept this critical slice of life.

Burns's cutthroat, selfish personality may also contribute to his discontent. He is not a "team player" by any definition of the phrase. For example, take the situation in "Team Homer," in which he wants to join the Pin Pals:

Burns: Listen here…I want to join your team.
Homer: You want to join my *what?*
Smithers: You want to *what* his team?
Burns: I've had one of my unpredictable changes of heart. Seeing these fine young athletes, reveling in the humiliation of a vanquished foe…mmm, I haven't felt this energized since my last… er…boweling.

(Later, after winning the championship)
Homer: Woo hoo! We won! We won!
Burns: You mean, *I* won.
Apu: But we were a team, sir.
Burns: Oh, I'm afraid I've had one of my trademark changes of heart. You see, teamwork will only take you so far. Then, the truly evolved person makes that extra grab for personal glory. Now, I must discard my

teammates, much like the boxer must shed roll after roll of sweaty, useless, disgusting flab before he can win the title. Ta! (He leaves.)

Burns's lack of camaraderie with his teammates coupled with his inherently selfish nature alienates him from other members of society. Burns might attain momentary happiness, but in the long run he cannot achieve true happiness without the friendship of others.

Burns's realization of his infirmities also contributes to his lack of happiness. For example, in "The Springfield Files," in which Burns is mistaken for an alien, he states, "A lifetime of being in a nuclear power plant has left me with a healthy green glow — and has left me as impotent as the Nevada boxing commissioner." Thus, Burns's lack of happiness is rooted both psychologically and physiologically. He realizes that he is impotent, and is mentally distraught by the concept. Since the actual cause of this stress is physiological, Burns has a legitimate reason to be distraught: he is inadequate as a man (sexually). While Burns is content that he is extremely wealthy, he is also upset that he cannot enjoy the pleasures (and perhaps duties, from a religious perspective) that most human beings carry out. Burns's lack of happiness is partially rooted in his incapacity to perform the same functions as other individuals. In reality, what Burns truly desires is to be like everyone else (in matters of love, sex, performing everyday tasks). He despises these shortcomings, and thus can never be truly happy.

Finally, further evidence of Burns's lack of true happiness comes from the fact that he occasionally engages in activities orchestrated to relate to the "common" man. Burns's participation in the following events serve to support this thesis: Burns comes over to the Simpson home to watch the big fight, joins the Pin Pals, and drinks beers with Homer at Isotopes games. In one episode, Burns talks with Homer, and effectively lowers himself to the common man: "Oh, yes, sitting—the great leveler. From the mightiest pharaoh to the lowliest peasant, who doesn't enjoy a good sit?"

Furthermore, it may be argued that Burns experiences his happiest moment when Smithers is on vacation, and he must drive a car, answer a telephone, and shop in a supermarket by himself. Burns tends to be happiest when he is not "himself." Thus, he does indeed lack the ideal of true happiness.

CHAPTER 7

The Practice of Dr. Hibbert versus the Malpractice of Dr. Nick (and a Small Dose of Dr. Steve)

"Don't worry, Marge. America's health care system is second only to Japan, Canada, Sweden, Great Britain, well, all of Europe, but you can thank your lucky stars we don't live in Paraguay!"[*]

— *Homer*

Medical doctors are portrayed in strikingly different manners on *The Simpsons*. For example, the Simpson family generally relies heavily on their trusted family doctor, Dr. Julius Hibbert. Hibbert at times seems to be a serious, well-intentioned doctor. However, his numerous outbursts of laughter at inappropriate moments certainly serve to counter this point. Dr. Nick, on the other hand, is a charlatan — a quack, a pretender of knowledge. Dr. Nick may not burst into fits of laughter, but he certainly does not take his job seriously. Case and point: Dr. Nick once admitted to using a knife and fork in the operating room ("22 Short Films About Springfield"):

---

[*] http://www.snpp.com/other/papers/bv.paper.html

Dr. Nick: Hi, everybody!

The Board: Hi, Dr. Nick.

Board Chairman: Dr. Nick, this malpractice committee has received a few complaints against you. Of the 160 gravest charges, the most troubling are performing major operations with a knife and fork from a seafood restaurant...

Dr. Nick: But I cleaned them with my napkin!

Board chairman: ...misuse of cadavers

Dr. Nick: I get here earlier when I drive in the carpool lane!

It is to the practice of Dr. Hibbert versus the malpractice of Dr. Nick that we now turn.

The Practice of Dr. Hibbert

Dr. Hibbert encompasses many of the qualities of the classic family doctor. For example, he is intelligent, kind (most of the time), and does not tolerate nonsense. Hibbert's business-like approach is exemplified when he discusses his price for Homer's snoring surgery:

Dr. Hibbert: This is what it costs. (Scribbles down a figure and hands it to Homer.)

Homer: Hmm... here's my counter offer. (Writes something.)

(Dr. Hibbert reads the note. It reads, "Do it for free.")

Dr. Hibbert (laughs as usual, but then becomes serious): Get out.

This example is important to consider because many doctors in contemporary society similarly work "only for the money." In this instance, both Hibbert's and Homer's comments were out of line. They should have negotiated further and found a middle ground. Unfortunately, the aforementioned situation is not uncommon in contemporary society. There are many instances in which patients do not receive the proper medical treatment because they can't afford the expenses. Thus, the aforementioned example serves as a reflection of certain medical practices (or lack thereof) in our society.

Still, *The Simpsons* does make the point that the American medical establishment is better than medical establishments set up in other countries. For example, the writers once ridiculed the healthcare system in Canada. When the Simpson family traveled to Toronto, Homer attempted to cross a busy street, only to be warned by Lisa not to do so. Homer's response was classic: "They have free healthcare here." Homer then gets hit by a car. He is flipped in the air, only to exclaim, "I'm rich!" By critiquing the healthcare system in Canada, the writers have demonstrated (subtly, perhaps) their inherent pride in the American healthcare system.

Let's return to our analysis of Dr. Hibbert for a moment. Since *The Simpsons* is a comedy, there are many instances in which Dr. Hibbert is utilized to produce humor. Most of these instances of humor do not take much away from the respectability of Dr. Hibbert as an established medical doctor. However, the following quotes and examples do serve to influence our perception of Dr. Hibbert in a negative way:

★ When Homer lost his thumb, Hibbert suggested cutting off the other thumb for a sense of symmetry.

★ Marge: Is it safe [for Homer] to eat that much food, Dr. Hibbert?
  Dr. Hibbert: You know, I wouldn't have thought so before I bought 12% of this restaurant, but now, I feel a balanced diet can include the occasional eating contest." (Rex then dies from eating too much steak!)
  — *"Maximum Homerdrive"*

★ Dr. Hibbert leaves Hans Moleman in the X-ray machine, and goes home.

Dr. Hibbert's Humor

★ Dr. Hibbert attends to a shaking Carl, holding a Grandma Plopwell's pudding cup in "They Saved Lisa's Brain."

Dr. Hibbert: Do you suffer from diabetes?
Carl: No.
Dr. Hibbert: Well, you do now. (Hibbert breaks into his classic laughter.)

★ Dr. Hibbert, to Marge: "I'm afraid your husband is dead. Just kidding."

★ Grampa: How long do I have to live, Doc?
Dr. Hibbert (laughs): I'm amazed you're alive now.

★ Ned (running into Dr. Hibbert, who is near the post office): Get your taxes out of the way?
Dr. Hibbert: No, just mailing out death certificates for holiday-related fatalities, ah-heh, heh, heh.

★ Dr. Hibbert, in "Make Room for Lisa": "When it comes to stress, I believe laughter is the best medicine. You know, before I learned to chuckle mindlessly, I was headed for an early grave myself. Ah, heh, heh, heh."

★ After Bart got injured in a comedic fashion, Hibbert showed the Simpson family other comedy-related injuries: "We call them 'traumedies'. Those guys crack me up."

In these instances, Dr. Hibbert's sense of humor certainly translates into insensitivity.

The Dr. Hibbert Chuckle

What Simpsons fan has not attempted to laugh like Dr. Hibbert? Hibbert's laugh defines his character so much so that Nelson Muntz once deceived cops by claiming to be Dr. Hibbert. When the police apologized for supposedly mistaking his identity (they correctly knew that Nelson is a thug), Nelson mimicked Dr. Hibbert's chuckle and said he forgave the cops for initially questioning his identity.

Dr. Hibbert's laugh represents the lightheartedness (if not carefree) demeanor of many contemporary American medical doctors. For instance, I have heard some doctors attempt to convince patients to lose weight. A classic method: "You don't want to be a blimp," followed by a Dr. Hibbert-like chuckle. To be sure, many doctors do not display such a sense of humor. Still, the writers of *The Simpsons* have picked up on a small detail found in the personalities of some contemporary American doctors.

As Dr. Hibbert himself once noted, his chuckle serves as a remedy for stress. Dr. Hibbert teaches all of us that a little laughter goes a long way in relieving stress. Late-night comedians such as Jay Leno use laughter as an effective means of relieving the inevitable stress that comes along with national politics. By ridiculing O.J. Simpson, Bill Clinton, and President Bush (#43), Leno transforms serious situations into comedic drama. Perhaps Leno and Letterman have been talking to Dr. Hibbert

The Malpractice of Dr. Nick Riviera

You've been in a car accident. You want to "ching ching ching" cash in on your injury. Who do you call? Well, if you're a resident of Springfield, you'd probably first call Lionel Hutz. Then you'd call a doctor to receive a written description of your injuries. So do you call Dr. Hibbert or Dr. Nick?

Well, let's examine what the Simpson family did when Bart was hit by a car in a Season 2 episode entitled "Bart Gets Hit By a Car." After Bart was hit by Mr. Burns's "luxury car of death," the family hires Lionel Hutz as their attorney. Hutz gives the family the following advice pertaining to doctors: "Doctors! Pffft! Doctors are idiots...you can ching-ching-ching cash in on this tragedy." Thus, Hutz brings the family to visit Dr. Nick.

Dr. Nick examines Bart and discusses Bart's injuries with the rest of the family:

> Dr Nick: Your son is a very sick boy. Just look at these X-rays! (He holds up a large X-ray of Bart's head, spikey hair and all). You see that dark spot there? Whiplash.
> Homer: Whiplash! Oh no!
> Dr. Nick: And this smudge that looks like my fingerprint? No. That's trauma.
> Dr. Nick (wrapping bandages around Bart's head), to Hutz: Just say when.

Dr. Nick in this episode does not merely act irresponsibly: he acts recklessly. He and Hutz attempt to deceive the jury into believing Bart's injuries are worse then they actually are. But Burns's lawyers aren't fooled by the misstatements. When Burns's lawyers question Marge as to how she feels about Dr. Hibbert, Marge responds honestly: "He's been our family physician and trusted friend ever since I've been a mother." When questioned as to what she thinks of Dr. Nick, she responds: "[Dr. Nick] seemed a lot more concerned about wrapping Bart in bandages than about making him feel better; he mispronounced words...now that I think about it, I'm not sure he's even a doctor." She is correct in her assertion that Dr. Nick is a quack.

In fact, Dr. Nick is the definition of a quack. His lack of seriousness, unlike Dr. Hibbert's occasional lapses of levity, is completely unacceptable. Dr. Nick's motive for his recklessness isn't necessarily directly related to personal financial gain (although he did once remark, after performing work on Mr. Burns: "the most rewarding part was when he gave me my money.") Still, other than perhaps a few isolated incidents, Dr. Nick does not discuss financial matters. True, Dr. Nick may try to cut certain corners in attempts to save money, but his mishaps seem to be more directly related to his poor education than to his goal of achieving financial success. Recall that Dr. Nick attended "Hollywood Upstairs Medical College," the "Club Med School," and the "Mayo Clinic Correspondence School."

The Role of Dr. Nick

Dr. Nick's most important role is in episodes which center on potential medical disasters. In "King-Size Homer," for instance, Dr. Nick advises Homer on how to gain weight quickly:

Dr. Nick: You'll want to focus on the neglected food groups, such as the whipped group, the congealed group, and the choc-o-tastic.

Homer: What can I do to speed the whole thing up, doctor?

Dr. Nick: Well, be creative. Instead of making sandwiches with bread, use Pop-Tarts. Instead of chewing gum, chew bacon.

Bart: You could brush your teeth with milkshakes!

Dr. Nick: Hey, did you go to Hollywood Upstairs Medical College, too? And remember, if you're not sure about something, rub it against a piece of paper. If the paper turns clear, it's your window to weight gain.

.. In "Homer's Triple Bypass":

"Now if something should go wrong, let's not get the law involved. One hand washes the other."

.. And the last thing Homer hears from Dr. Nick before going under the anesthesia:

"What the hell is that?"

.. In "Round Springfield," Dr. Nick prepares Bart for surgery:

"Whoopsie. Heh. Maybe if I fiddle with these knobs...Hey, I smell gas. Pleasant gas. Night-night gas."

.. In "Treehouse of Horror IX," Homer goes to Dr. Nick for a hair transplant:

Homer: This is legal, right?
Dr. Nick: Yeah, sure, whatever.

.. In "Trilogy of Error":

"Inflammable means flammable? What a country!"

Other memorable quotes from Dr. Nick:

.. Dr. Nick, about a pregnant woman: That lady swallowed a baby?

.. And what *Simpsons* fan could ever forget Dr. Nick's 'knee-bone' song?

"The knee-bone's connected to the something.
The something's connected to the red thing.
The red-thing's connected to my wrist watch—uh oh!"

Hi Everybody!

If nothing else, Dr. Nick is friendly. He loves to greet everyone he meets, from his patients to strangers on the street to Mel Gibson. In one memorable scene, for instance, Dr. Nick greets a former patient: "Well, if it isn't Mr. McCraig: the man with a leg for an arm and an arm for a leg!" (Of course, the man's deformities were a direct result of Dr. Nick's mistakes during a surgical procedure).

It is important for medical doctors in contemporary society to be people-friendly. People skills are incredibly important in the medical establishment. In the movie *Patch Adams*, for example, Patch Adams, played by Robin Williams, is extremely gentle and kind to patients in the hospital. He correctly remarks that medical books don't have the power to make patients feel happy. If people are treated well, he argues, their chances of recovery will improve. Dr. Nick's friendliness, therefore, would go a long way—that is, if he combined his people skills with actual medical knowledge (which he obviously lacks).

A Small Dose of Dr. Steve: It's Chirotown

In the episode entitled "Pokey Mom," Homer incurs a back injury. He first sees Dr. Hibbert who tells him modern medicine has a lousy record of treating the back. "We spend too much time on the front." Dr. Hibbert recommends that Homer see a chiropractor (Dr. Steve). Homer then questions Dr. Hibbert's recommendation:

Dr. Hibbert: I'm going to send you to my chiropractor.
Homer: Hey, I thought real doctors hated chiropractors.
Dr. Hibbert: Well, that is our official stance, but between you, me, and my golf clubs, they're miracle workers.

Homer then visits Dr. Steve, and is given a minor adjustment. Homer notes that his back feels a little better. Dr. Steve then tells Homer that he'll have to "see [him] three times a week for, uh...many, many years." This quote examines the perceived nature of chiropractors in contemporary society: they want to attract and KEEP customers.

Later in the episode, Homer accidentally invents the "Spine-O-Cylinder," a garbage can that is indented in such a way that it magically cures back problems. As Homer starts to attract patients, chiropractors lose business. A few chiropractors break into Homer's garbage, and destroy the Spine-O-Cylinder.

Homer notes the irony of the situation in a conversation with Dr. Steve:

> Dr. Steve: Simpson! You're not a licensed chiropractor, and you're stealing patients from me and from Dr. Steffi.
> Homer: Boy, talk about irony. The AMA tries to drive you guys out of business, now you're doing the same to me. Think about the irony.
> Steve (grabs Homer by the collar): You've been warned. Stop chiropracting.
> Homer: Not unless you *think about the irony.*

It is interesting to note Homer's brilliant commentary on medical doctors and chiropractors. What we realize is that the medical establishment is a business. If nobody ever became ill, medical doctors would lose most of their business. Similarly, if anyone ever develops a magical "Spine-O-Cylinder," chiropractors would have a difficult time attracting — and keeping — customers.

One final note

The Simpsons is unique in that it attacks and/or supports virtually every professional career in contemporary society. Medical malpractice is a serious issue in America, and *The Simpsons* serves an important role in discussing the issue in an open manner (via Dr. Nick). Still, we do believe that most doctors are qualified—even if many of those qualified have various character flaws (such as laughing at inappropriate times). Now give me a Dr. Hibbert chuckle...

CHAPTER 8

The Minor Characters

"Producers fiddle with shows all the time; they change characters, drop others, and push some into the background." *(We then see Mr. Largo and the Capital City Goofball walk by the Simpson window.)*

— Lisa

I'd like to take some time to devote a section of this book to the lesser-known characters. These characters are important for several reasons. Firstly, the surplus of characters on *The Simpsons* has contributed to the longevity of the series. Many plots and storylines have centered on some of these lesser-known characters. Secondly, each character has a defining role in the community (Moe the Bartender, Comic Book Guy, Gil the Salesman). These characters serve to attract viewers from every sphere: policemen will laugh at Chief Wiggum's antics, and salesmen will smile at Gil's numerous misfortunes.

I've grouped many characters into the following lists: *The Stars, Almost Famous: Minor Stars, Twenty two Minutes of Fame, and the Oft-Forgotten characters.* Please note that I have not listed every single Simpson character on these lists, as that would be nearly impossible. I have not listed most of the insignificant characters who have appeared on the show for a few seconds. Still, I have listed most, if not all, of the popular characters on the series. Please also note that I have used *The Simpsons Guide Books* to help compile these lists, and thus several characters that first appeared during seasons 13 and 14 may not appear on the lists.

Every human being (hermits excluded) comes into contact with hundreds of persons throughout the course of his or her life. We focus on some of these individuals and form relationships with them. Other individuals seem less relevant in our lives, and we tend to ignore or forget about them. For example, an employee in a large office building cannot possibly form relationships with every person he sees. Thus, the pushing aside of minor and often-forgotten characters on *The Simpsons* serves as a reflection of person-to-person relationships in contemporary society. The introduction of minor characters also adds another dimension to the series; that being that Springfield is composed of different types of people. The abundance of characters on the series enables us to view Springfield as a realistic town. Just as we pop into our local hardware store perhaps once every couple of years, so too do the writers of *The Simpsons* give a small amount of air time to minor characters. Fans of the series are aware that these characters exist in Springfield, but they are often irrelevant to most aspects of the episodes.

The Stars:

Homer
Marge
Bart
Lisa
Maggie

Almost Famous: Minor Stars

Michael Idato highlighted Al Jean's comments in his article entitled "Ready, set, d'oh!":

"One thing that has changed, however, is the growth of the show's supporting cast. Originally, Castellaneta, Kavner, Cartwright and Smith were hired to play the Simpson family, and the show didn't venture far beyond, respectively, Homer, Marge, Bart and Lisa. Now the supporting cast numbers more than 100, and characters like Barney Gumble, Moe, Chief Wiggum, Waylon Smithers and Ned Flanders have loyal followings among the fans.

"Definitely from the second year there was an increase [in] the size of the Simpson universe," says Al Jean. "We would explore who Patty and Selma might know, or how Burns related to Smithers. [One of the keys] to the longevity of the series is that there are about 30 or 40 characters that people are really attached to, many of whom were there in the first year, and some of whom were even in the shorts, like Krusty or Grandpa. There is no question that it enables the show to stay fresh, having so many characters."[*]

These characters serve as the supporting cast of the series. Many episode plots center on the characters listed below. Many of the characters listed below have had numerous encounters with the Simpson family.

Mr. Burns
Krusty the Clown

---

[*] http://www.smh.com.au/articles/2003/02/26/1046064102384.html

Ned Flanders
Rainier Wolfcastle
Agnus Skinner
Luigi
Disco Stu
Kearney
Cletus
Hans Moleman
Troy McClure
Waylon Smithers
Snake
Judge Snyder
Burns's blue-Haired lawyer
Santa's Little Helper
Snowball II
Martin Prince
Jimbo Jones
Edna Krabappel
Todd Flanders
Rod Flanders
Kent Brockman
Lionel Hutz
Principal Skinner
Reverend Lovejoy
Comic Book Guy
Dr. Julius Hibbert
Dr. Nick Riviera
Fat Tony
Legs
Louie
Johnny Tightlips
Nelson Muntz
Moe Szyslak
Lenny
Carl Carlson

Groundskeeper Willie
Mr. Teeny
Lou
Eddie
Otto the bus driver
Selma Bouvier
Patty Bouvier
Milhous Van Houten
Professor Frink
Abe Simpson
Sideshow Bob
Sideshow Mel
Dolph
Kirk Van Houten
Louanne Van Houten
God
The Devil
Radioactive Man
Itchy
Scratchy
Barney Gumble
Chief Clancy Wiggum
Apu
Ralph Wiggum
Pimple-faced kid
Crazy Old Man
Sherri
Terri
Captain McCalister
Bumblebee Man
Manjula
Superintendent Chalmers
Mayor Quimby
Raphael (Sarcastic Man)
Database

Gil
Jasper
Kang
Kodos
Mrs. Lovejoy
Mrs. Wiggum
Mrs. Hibbert
Duffman
Brandine Del Roy
Malibu Stacy
Mrs. Hoover
Arnie Pye
The Rich Texan
Lindsey Naegle

The Oft-Forgotten Characters

Some of the characters on this list played fundamental roles at some point during the series' run. However, the writers chose not to fully develop these characters. Other characters on this list seemed to be potentially prominent characters, but never received the airtime to "prove" themselves. (It may be argued that characters such as Mrs. Wiggum and Mrs. Hibbert should be on this list because they do not play fundamental roles on the series. However, they are somewhat important because they are both married to popular *Simpsons* characters, Clancy Wiggum, and Dr. Hibbert, respectively.)

Herman
Capital City Goofball
Mr. Largo
Mrs. Bouvier

Uter
Janey
Wendell
Louis
Lunchlady Doris
Bill (KBBL)
Marty (KBBL)

Deceased

The fact that the writers of *The Simpsons* have killed off several characters serves to make the series more realistic. (By contrast, how many characters died on *The Flintstones?*) None of these characters played an extremely important role on the series, but the avid fan certainly was aware of their existence in the community.

Dr. Marvin Monroe
Frank Grimes
Cornelius Chapman (108-year-old Springfield resident)
Bleeding Gums Murphy
Maude Flanders
Snowball I

Twenty-two Minutes of Fame

These characters, for the most part, have made only one or two appearances on the series. (There are some exceptions.) Many of these characters were voiced by guest stars, which would serve to explain why they have appeared on the show so infrequently. Still, each of these characters played a fundamental role on the episode in which they starred. For twenty-two minutes (the approximate length of a *Simpsons* episode), many of these characters had the spotlight.

Bob (owner of Bob's RV Roundup)
Jacques
Princess Kashmir
Ugolin
Cesar
Karl (Homer's assistant)
Ms. Botz
Blinky
Captain Lance Murdock
Roger Meyers
Akira
Artie Ziff (two episodes)
Herb Powell (two episodes)
Emily Winthrop
Bea Simmons
Professor Lombardo
General Sherman
Mr. Bergstrom
Leon Kompowsky
Congressman Bob Arnold
Rabbi Krustofski (starred in one episode, appeared briefly
    in a Season 14 episode)
Hugo
Millicent
Woodrow (Edna's crush)
Lurleen Lumpkin
Mother Simpson
Laddie
Llewellyn Sinclair
Amber Dempsey
Laura Powers

Ruth Powers (two episodes)
Homer's relatives
Lyle Lanley
Pepi
Gabbo (starred in one episode, appeared briefly in a second episode)
Arthur Crandall
Brad Goodman
Mindy Simmons
Molloy
Stacy Lovell
Stampy
Jessica Lovejoy
Ashley Grant
Number One
Evan Conover
Don Vittorio
Little Vicki Valentine
Ballet Teacher (not given a name)
Freak Show Manager (not given a name)
Freddy Quimby
Allison Taylor
Birch Barlow
Hugh Parkfield
Shelby
Jericho
Jimmy
Arman Tamzarian
Lard-O-Lad marketing ad (came alive in a Halloween episode)
Colonel Leslie Hapablap
Cecil
Detective Don Brodka (from Try-N-Save store)
Larry Burns
Cooder

Spud
Hollis Hurlbut
Chester J. Lampwick
Poochie
The [Grizzly] Bear
Erin
Rachel Jordan (appeared in at least two episodes)
Ak
Qtokotok
Casino Manager
The Southern Sheriff
Becky
St. Peter
Sophie
Frankie the Squealer
Christopher Walken (as himself)
Jesse Grass
Jebediah Springfield
Number Six
Fake Homer
Bobo
Devon Bradley
Jack Crowley
Lieutenant L.T. Smash
Howard K. Duff VIII
Francine (Lisa's bully)
Kitenge
Thelonious (boy at West Springfield Elementary)
Wolfcastle's daughter
Singing Railroad Hobo
Wally Kogen
Homer Simpson, Police Cop
Señor Ding Dong
Stuart the Duck
Astrid Weller

Arthur Fortune (billionaire)
Chuck Garabedian
Mezmerino
Brother Faith
Linguo
Funzo
Ramrod
Meathook
Apu's mother
Larry Kidkill
The Southern Colonel
Lifeways Editor
Edward Christian
Roy
Commandant
"Lisa" (Lisa's replacement in the Spin-off showcase episode)
Seth
Mr. Sparkle
Rex Banner
John (gay man)
Shary Bobbins
Frank Ormand, The Pretzel Man
Coyote
Dr. Foster (Ned's doctor)
Belle
Lucius Sweet
Hank Scorpio
Drederick Tatum (has now appeared in several episodes)
The Leader
Renee
Captain Tenille
Mojo the helper monkey
Ray Patterson
Brad (Powersauce marketer)

Neil (Powersauce marketer)
Alex Whitney
Chirpy Boy (lizard)
Bart Jr. (lizard)
Jub-Jub
Munchie
Mr. Pinchy
Leavelle
Amber (Vegas wife, two episodes)
Ginger (Vegas wife, two episodes)
Apu's octuplets: Poonam, Sashi, Sandeep, Uma, Anoop, Pria, Gheet, Nabendu

CHAPTER 9

The Simpsons Versus Other Television Sitcoms

"Thank you Bill Cosby, you saved the Simpsons!"
— *Homer ["Saturdays of Thunder"]*

"Simpson, Homer Simpson, he's the greatest guy in his-
to-ry. From the town of Springfield, he's about to hit a
chestnut tree. D'oh!"
— *Homer, singing to the tune of The Flintsones theme song*

Ed Bishop of *The Riverfront Times* pointedly notes that *The
Simpsons* is a revolutionary show:

"I know other shows on television are funny. But the
appeal of *The Simpsons* goes beyond its humor. There's
an angst, a kind of doom, in *The Simpsons* that's unlike
anything else on television. The Simpsons are a family
of losers and they know it. Homer and Marge will
never get beyond their debts and the middle-class
values they actually hate. Lisa will grow up and marry
someone like her father, never opening up the poet
inside her. Bart will likely die in a drag-racing accident. Yet, though there's angst and even self-pity in
these characters, they are not defeated. Their aware-
ness of their limitations and their struggle against
them are a rare combination for television sit-coms. ...

On *The Simpsons*, it's the world that's dysfunctional. In other words, unlike the narrative neatness on even the best TV shows, these cartoon characters have a reality about them. A kind of joy exists in that."[*]

How does *The Simpsons* match up against other television sitcoms? Every sitcom has its own agenda at hand, and thus it is interesting to examine the fundamental similarities and differences between *The Simpsons* and other television sitcoms of the 20th century.

The Role of the TV Husband

Several immediate similarities can be found between the role of the husband in many television sitcoms. For example, Homer Simpson often goes to Moe's Tavern to get out and away from his family. As Homer once remarked: "To Marge, and all the blissful years I've spent hiding from her in this bar." Similarly, Dan's (from *Roseanne*) favorite beverage is beer.[†] Additionally, Fred Flintstone and Ralph Cramden share similarities with Homer, as they often went bowling at night, and were both members of a club. (Homer has attempted to join the Stonecutters. Homer also enjoys bowling: in one episode he bowled a perfect 300 game).

The adult male figure in many sitcoms has the following characteristics: fat, lazy, enjoys beer, and is generally a good guy. For example, Fred Flintstone and Ralph Cramden, despite their sharp tempers, are well-intentioned individuals. Ralph, on *The Honeymooners*, wants nothing more than to earn more money so that he and his wife can life a more luxurious lifestyle. Each of the aforementioned figures (Fred Flintstone, Ralph Cramden, Homer Simpson, and Dan Con-

---

* Article found at The Simpsons Archive: www.snpp.com
† Terrace, Vincent. *Television Sitcom Fact Book.* United States: McFarland and Company, Inc., 2000.

ner) love their wives, but at times feel constrained by the borders of their homes. Thus, the adult male figure in these sitcoms feels the need to join a club outside of their home.

The general consensus among the aforementioned male figures pertaining to the membership in clubs is a reflection of adult male figures in contemporary society. For example, many married adult men join bowling leagues, social clubs, play poker (just as Dan Conner plays poker), or drink beer. Each sitcom portrays marriage as rewarding, but challenging at times. The social clubs and poker games enable the adult male figure to free himself, for a short duration, from the frequent struggles and challenges that inevitably come with married life. None of the figures mentioned above gets a divorce from their female counterpart. Perhaps the reason for this is that they set aside time for themselves, and when they return home, they can more easily concentrate on overcoming the challenges (and reaping the benefits) of married life. Their social outlets (bowling, poker) eliminate some of the stresses of married life. Perhaps the balance of work and pleasure is the key to sustaining a successful marriage.[*]

The Role of the TV Wife

"If I wasn't a housewife, I think I'd be a homemaker, or maybe a domestic engineer."

— Marge Simpson

The role of the conventional television wife is also important to consider. It may be argued that Marge Simpson's character is an amalgamation of previous TV wives from June Cleaver, Alice Cramden, Wilma Flintstone, and Edith

---

[*] Also note that Archie Bunker in *All in The Family* often goes to Kelsey's Bar to "escape" from household feuds and his frustrations with the Bunker clan.

Bunker to the likes of more recent TV wives such as Peg Bundy. The role of the TV wife in sitcoms that aired before 1980 was to take care of her children and to support her husband. As society has progressed, and many married women now work, so too has TV reflected these changes. For example, Marge once attempted to begin a career as a real-estate agent. However, for the most part, Marge is a stay-at-home wife. She has been known to have liberal views pertaining to the role of women in society: in high school, she spoke up for women's rights ("The Way We Was"). Still, Marge's character is not revolutionary; she is largely conventional.

Marge was certainly not the first TV wife to attempt to land a career. Lucy Ricardo, in *I Love Lucy*, constantly strived to be cast in Ricky's shows at the Tropicana club. In one episode, she also landed a job as a chocolate wrapper. And who could forget the famous "Vitameatavegamin" commercial she attempted to star in. Lucy was more revolutionary than Marge because she was one of the first—if not the first TV wife—to actually work outside of the home. As society has become more open-minded in their views pertaining to the role of women, TV wives began to work outside of the home. Marge's character combines the perceived complacency of June Cleaver with the motivation of revolutionaries such as Lucy.

Marge doesn't lack power in the Simpson household nor does she possess a lot of power. Although this statement may seem to contradict itself, let me explain what I mean. Let's examine *Roseanne*. Roseanne Conner had power. She was the queen in the Conner household. And she knew it. Conversely, Wilma Flintstone did not possess much power in the household. Her role was more traditional: cook, clean, take care of her family. Although Roseanne did also cook, clean, and take care of her family, she felt that, outside of those boundaries, she had the power to make important decisions. For example, she decided to purchase a restaurant (which served loose meat sandwiches) with her sister Jackie. It's difficult to envision Wilma opening up a restaurant.

Now here's why the issue of power in the household is not relevant in our discussion of *The Simpsons*. Marge can do anything she wants—Homer won't stop her. Still, her approach is more laid back: she is content being a housewife, and although she occasionally pursues other interests (painting, real estate), she is happy with the way things are. Thus, she is the paradigm of the modern housewife in contemporary society. She doesn't *have* to be a housewife –she *wants* to be a housewife. And she teaches us that there is nothing wrong with that; perhaps it is admirable. She places her family above all else, and has fun while doing so. Marge once noted that she prepares several meals before she serves dinner in order to practice. She knows that her job is important, and she is content with her role as the contemporary TV housewife.

Bill Cosby versus *The Simpsons*

The Simpsons' portrayal of Bill Cosby (not actually voiced by Bill Cosby):

"[Kids today] listen to the rap music that causes the brain damage, with their bippen' and a boppin' and they're trippin' and a hoppin', so they don't know what the jazz is all about. You see, jazz is like Jello pudding—no wait, it's more like Kodak film—no wait, it's more like the common cold: it will never go away."

Bill Cosby: Now my good man, what do you like to play?
Kid: Pokemon!
Bill Cosby: Pokemon!? Pokemon with the poke and the mon and the thing where the guy comes out of the thing, and he makes a fraaagh fr fra aagh aagh aagh!
Homer: Hehe—kids say the darndest things!

What was Fox thinking when they decided to air *The Simpsons* on Thursday nights at 8 P.M. opposite *The Cosby Show*? *The Cosby Show* had it all—talented and likeable characters, interesting storylines, and, perhaps most importantly, a large audience. Still, Fox's decision to air a prime-time cartoon during the same time slot as *The Cosby Show* obviously paid off big time.

The Simpsons has had a longer run than *The Cosby Show*. Perhaps this has to do with the fact that real actors are required to produce non-animated sitcoms. When publications such as *Time* and *TV Guide* started to compare *The Cosby Show* with *The Simpsons*, they only added fuel to the fire. *The Simpsons* eventually moved to its current time slot: Sundays at 8 PM. The series is Fox's third highest rated show, while *The Cosby Show* is frequently aired on Nick-at-Nite. It's unfair to say that *The Simpsons* beat *The Cosby Show*, but the prime-time cartoon certainly made a name for itself by successfully competing against such a popular series.

Prime-Time Parenting

It would be exceedingly difficult to argue that Bill Cosby was portrayed as a sub-par father on *The Cosby Show*. In most instances, he tries to resolve issues with his children in the proper manner, teaches morals to his children, and acts as the ideal father in many situations. Dr. Huxtable won the respect of his children because he took the aforementioned measures. His children certainly would not dare call him by his first name, Cliff. Conversely, both Lisa and Bart have referred to their father as Homer, although they do also at times call him dad. (Lisa, in fact, generally refers to her father as dad, but has, at times, called him Homer.) Parental respect is an important issue in contemporary society, and the writers of both *The Simpsons* and *The Cosby Show* were well aware of this truth. Still, their approaches to the issue at hand were strikingly different.

The writers of *The Simpsons* decided to address the issue of respect for one's parents in a unique but interesting manner. In sharp contrast to critics' comments that *The Simpsons* fosters a lack of respect, it may be argued that *The Simpsons* may actually encourage respect for parents. Here's why: the influence of the series pertaining to the matter of respect depends on the audience at hand. Of course, if young children are watching the series, they will most certainly try to imitate the actions of Bart. However, *The Simpsons* is intended for a more mature audience (it is the highest rated sitcom on Sunday nights for males between the ages of 18-49). For older audiences, the lack of respect displayed by Bart in the earlier years of the series' run serves as comedy in its purest form. Many of Homer's parenting techniques, which are examined in Chapter 1 of this volume, are certainly not praiseworthy. However, *The Simpsons* portrays the average American family correctly: not every father is a great father. *The Cosby Show* creates the illusion that families always run into problems that can be quickly resolved. In addition, *The Cosby Show* creates the sense that children always behave in manners that are quickly correctable with the proper utilization of parenting techniques. *The Simpsons*, on the other hand, addresses the issue of behavior by showing that parents often cannot control their children. (Homer often cannot control Bart's behavior, and, out of frustration, chokes Bart. Somehow I find it hard to imagine Dr. Huxtable choking young Rudy when she gets in trouble).

Examples of Dr. Huxtable's Parenting Techniques[*]

★ "I brought you into this world, and I can take you out."

★ "Your mother and I are rich; you have nothing."

★ "A long, long time ago, three to four generations ago, parents didn't talk much to their children. At four A.M, the father would come home, look at his son sleeping, wake him up and say 'Boy, go out and plough the field now.' And the boy would rub his eye and say 'Yes, pa.' And occasionally, the son would ask the father how much he'd get paid. And the father grabbed the plough, and ran over his son. Those days are over, because we have become more civilized, more sophisticated, but it's still inside of me no matter how sophisticated I get. And it grows over time. Boy, when I say to one of my children to do something and they say 'How much does it pay?' I think I'm going to buy a plough."

★ "No boy should have a $95 shirt unless he is onstage with his four brothers!"

★ "You know, America is a great place, but it doesn't have a place where you can get rid of your kids." *(This reminds me of something Homer would probably say.)*

In these situations, Dr. Huxtable gains the complete attention of his children. He is well respected. Thus, *The Cosby Show* provides the American audience with what they *desire*; *The Simpsons,* conversely, provides the public with what *is*.

---

[*] All quotes from The Cosby Show were found at: http://www.imdb.com/Quotes?0086687.

SECTION 2

Simpsonian Themes: The Simpsons On

Each of the following themes present in contemporary society has, at some point, been examined on *The Simpsons*. The following pages discuss fundamental issues such as politics, the Age of Television, Descartes' Three-Fold Method of Doubt, and the modern industrialized employee. Please note the vital impact that *The Simpsons* has had on society pertaining to several academic areas of study (politics, mass media, American Exceptionalism, philosophy, and industrialization). Also note that the following individual essays focus on central academic themes, and later tie these themes in with examples from *The Simpsons*. Since the writers of *The Simpsons* study society, it behooves us to analyze the following issues, and then explore how *The Simpsons* has treated each issue over the course of its prime time run.

CHAPTER 10

The Importance of Cartoons in Contemporary Society

Cartoons can serve as an important form of political discourse. *The Simpsons* is a series that explores virtually every realm of society. However, other cartoons also serve as a source of political commentary. It is time for society to realize the inherent value of cartoons, and their influence in contemporary culture.

Cartoons and Global Politics: Animation as a Source of Contemporary Commentary on World Affairs

"This nation [the United States] — in world war and in Cold War — has never permitted the brutal and lawless to set history's course. Now, as before, we will secure our nation, protect our freedom, and help others to find freedom of their own."
— *President George W. Bush, during his speech on Iraq, October 7, 2002*[*]

[*] Bush's Speech on War with Iraq: http://www.atour.com/government/usa/20030116b.html

Robin: Boy! That was our closest call ever! I have to admit that I was pretty scared!
Batman: I wasn't scared in the least.
Robin: Not at all?
Batman: Haven't you noticed how we always escape the vicious ensnarements of our enemies?
Robin: Yeah, because we're smarter than they are!
Batman: I like to think it's because our hearts are pure.[*]

> *— from the 1966 Batman television series,*
> *which was based on a cartoon comic strip*

Society has undergone many changes since the advent of television. Television, being a universal medium through which information can pass, has helped news reporters reach many homes at once. However, television does not simply convey news to the public, as other programs are also broadcast to large numbers of people. Often, other types of programs — such as cartoons — serve to enhance our perceptions of the world around us. Cartoons that center on conflict (Superman vs. Lex Luthor, for example) can serve to represent conflicts actually taking place in contemporary society. While the circumstances and actual events taking place in the "real" world will vary from those depicted in cartoon storylines, the fundamental theme expressed in cartoon and global politics is identical: *good will always destroy evil.*

One important similarity between past and contemporary cartoons is that many contain intense action. For example, modern cartoons such as *Batman* and *Teenage Mutant Ninja Turtles* serve to enhance global perceptions of good and evil. (Most young children will be able to tell you that Batman is the good guy and the Joker is the bad guy). In many ways, cartoons are simply animated representations of global conflict. If the United States government were to produce a cartoon based on their international political affairs, they most certainly would portray Osama bin Laden as the evildoer.

---

[*] http://www.geocities.com/cicatrix_zero/batman.html

Cartoon fans can thus make the analogy between evildoers in contemporary society and villains in cartoons (Shredder in *Teenage Mutant Ninja Turtles*, Lex Luthor in *Superman*, Two-Face in *Batman* — just to cite a few examples). Villains in cartoons almost invariably possess the following traits: ruthlessness, ill intentions, rudeness, and the willingness to harm innocent people. All of these characteristics fit the persona of villains in contemporary society (think about Osama bin Laden once again).

Cartoons also portray the good guys with certain distinguishable traits. For example, let us examine the similarities between Popeye, the Ninja Turtles, Superman, and Batman. Each of the aforementioned cartoon characters is heroic. Additionally, they all possess the following traits: strength, patience, intelligence, good intentions, selfless, and are also particularly well mannered. The United States government, in its attempt to be perceived as heroic assiduously attempts to possess each of these characteristics. For example, in the war with Iraq, the United States attempted to be perceived as patient (Hans Blix's weapons inspections), smart and well-intentioned ("War is the correct approach"), selfless ("We're going to war in part because we want to help innocent Iraqi civilians"), and well-mannered (we did not want to go to war during times in which Muslims were celebrating sacred holidays). Thus, it seems as though the main goal of The United States in public relations was to present itself as the "hero." Indeed, just as Batman will inevitably thwart the Riddler's evil plans, the United States thwarted Saddam Hussein's perceived ability to cause mass destruction.

In examining the similarities between cartoon violence and global politics, we come to the realization that the conflict between good and evil will always remain a fundamental issue in the world. Just as the good guy almost always wins in battle in cartoons, virtuous leaders in the real world will also overcome their enemies. Still, pugnacious leaders will always continue to engage in war. The sad reality is that war and crime are what makes the news interesting. If all were good in the world, we wouldn't need to watch the news; instead we could simply turn on Cartoon Network in a quest to satiate our inherent violent dispositions. If there was no war, we might ask ourselves: "Who needs the news when we can simply watch cartoons?" Of course, I'm not saying that cartoon violence breeds "real" violence: I'm only writing this section to express my wish that the United States possessed superpowers...

Ay Carumba!
Simpsonian News and Views

Homer on voting: "I voted for Prell to go back to the old glass bottle. Then I became deeply cynical."

Homer: "See these? American donuts. Glazed, powdered, and raspberry-filled. Now, how's that for freedom of choice?"

Marge: "I'd expect that from a French poodle, but not from an American dog."

As I read last week's edition of *Time*, I noticed a commonality between most of the news issues discussed. Of course, the news itself isn't interconnected in terms of content, but many of the national and international stories have been discussed on television. I'm not talking about news reported on network or cable news programs—I'm talking about news that has been reported on *The Simpsons*.

Diehard fans of *The Simpsons* are well aware that the program is not an average cartoon. *The Simpsons* has explored every realm of society, including religion, politics, the arts, sports, alcohol, law, and current events. For example, in the political sphere, *The Simpsons'* writers have portrayed Mayor Quimby, whose voice is strikingly similar to those of the Kennedy family, as a womanizer and a corrupt politician. Other characters are also portrayed in a stereotypical sense as well (a fat, lazy Comic Book Guy, an uptight Principal Skinner, a nerdy Martin Prince, and a drugged-up bus driver, namely Otto, just to cite a few examples).

By means of an analysis of any episode of *The Simpsons*, the aforementioned is overtly obvious. However, *The Simpsons* is also skilled at reporting (and satirizing) current events in the news. For example, several years after the Gulf War was over, the writers drew a soldier on the battlefield that was about to kill Saddam — only to fail in her attempt as a result of Krusty the Clown's antics.

In the realm of politics, Sideshow Bob, who has been convicted of attempted murder several times, once remarked "society needs a cold-blooded Republican." Similarly, a Republican news channel on *The Simpsons* once reported that 92% of Democrats are gay. While these views involve political jokes, the ideas expressed on *The Simpsons* seem to even out over the years (although some have argued that *The Simpsons* is indeed more left-wing). *The Simpsons* pokes fun at both Republicans (fans will recall Rich Texan's "yee-haw" after chopping down trees), and extreme left-wing liberals (recall Jesse Grass's plea for Lisa to sit in a tree so that they wouldn't chop it down).

Any thorough examination of Simpsonian politics must include a consideration of the episode in which Homer beats up former President George Bush. Bush was portrayed as a stingy classical conservative, who did not enjoy Bart Simpson's Dennis the Menace-like antics. While *The Simpsons* incorporates politics into the series, the Bush administration incorporated *The Simpsons* into their politics! As George Bush once remarked, "We want American families to be a lot more like the *Waltons* and less like the *Simpsons*." The Simpsonian rebuttal (by Bart): We're like the *Waltons* too — we're also praying for the Depression to be over." The reason that *The Simpsons* will become the longest running series in television history (they've signed on for at least an additional two seasons) is due in large part to the fact that the writers are not afraid to comment on, and often attack, politics and individual politicians. Bush may very well have deserved Homer's bashing...

Politics also played a fundamental role in "Mr. Lisa Goes to Washington." In this episode, Lisa, who is a finalist in an essay contest, travels to Washington D.C., only to find corruption amongst politicians, specifically Congressman Bob Arnold's chicanery. She becomes angry, but when she reports the corruption to higher officials, their response is frantic, and serves as a Simpsonian classic: "A little girl is losing faith in democracy." The officials then bust the corrupt Congressman, and democracy resumes its proper function.

There is no news media program that can support and promote democracy in the way in which *The Simpsons* does on a weekly basis. To further examine this point, let us reflect on the following lines from Lisa's essay: "When America was born on the hot July day in 1776, the trees in Springfield Forest were tiny saplings trembling towards the sun, and as they were nourished by Mother Earth, so too did our fledgling nation find strength in the simple ideals of equality and justice. Who would have thought such mighty oaks or such a powerful nation could grow out of something so fragile, so pure?" Hmm...kind of difficult to remember that *The Simpsons* is just a cartoon, right?

The Simpsons is often at the forefront of controversy. For example, after Season 13's airing of the Brazil episode, the Brazilian government threatened to sue Fox unless they received an official apology from Fox. (Fox did apologize.) The episode did indeed poke fun at Brazil—Homer was kidnapped by an unlicensed taxi driver, Brazilian children were portrayed as thieves, and Brazilian children's television was depicted as containing graphic sexual elements. Still, despite the criticism that the episode received, the American virtue of free speech enables the episode to continue to be aired over and over again on Fox. Since *The Simpsons* is a cartoon, they do possess a sense of innocence that other TV programs do not. As Jay Leno put it: "Brazil is threatening to sue *The Simpsons* over last week's episode. The Simpsons could not be reached for comment BECAUSE THEY ARE CARTOONS!"

The Simpsons has also reported a great deal of news throughout their fourteen seasons. To list a few events: Michael Jackson dangling his baby, the downfall of dot.com companies, and, as the butt of one memorable joke, O.J. Simpson.

Homer: Wait a minute the white Bronco, the glove, the DNA evidence—O.J.'s guilty!

As long as there is news to report, *The Simpsons* will be there for satirical comment. So the next time you watch *The Simpsons*, try to pay particular attention to the intricate details that focus on news and politics. (There's a reason why former Pres. Bush was seen sitting at an execution service— and why former Pres. Clinton was seen dancing with Marge). As I finish this section, and slip into my Homer Simpson boxer shorts, I assure you that Simpsonian flavored politics have a lot to offer the American public. While you may not agree with a particular view expressed on *The Simpsons*, do the writers of the series one simple favor: Don't have a cow, man.

ESSAY # 1

Politics and the Typographic Mind

"In a culture dominated by print, public discourse tends to be characterized by a coherent, orderly arrangement of facts and ideas."

— *Neil Postman*, The Typographic Mind

Lisa Simpson: It's not our fault our generation has short attention spans, dad. We watch an appalling amount of TV.
Homer Simpson: Don't you EVER talk that way about television.[*]

Typographic America refers to the era in which the printed word monopolized the media industry. Widespread reading served an integral role in creating an atmosphere of rational thought in early America. High literacy rates spurred the development of the typographic mind as Americans began to believe that the reading process encourages rationality.[†] Rationality began to play an important role in politics as vot-

[*] One negative impact of television has been its reduction of the collective attention span of the American public in contemporary society. Modern-day intellectuals must consider whether or not they would be able to sit through the eight-hour Lincoln-Douglas debates.

101

ers read pamphlets and listened to debates between candidates running for political office. However, the advent of television stole some of the spotlight from the print media. Television continues to serve as a competitor in the news media field, but much of the news that television reports on is influenced by the printed media. For this reason, political newspapers still serve as the fountainhead of information in an age dominated by visual media.

In *Typographic America*[*], Neil Postman argues that the print media possessed a monopoly on the consciousness of the American people. Postman attributes the prodigious impact of print media to two major factors: high literacy rates (In New England, 89-95% of men could read or write; 65% of women were literate), and the fact that printed matter was virtually *all* that was available (p.41). Since print was the only medium through which information could be exchanged on a widespread basis, the news media was able to create a sense of national consciousness in the psyche of the American public. For example, the *Federalist Papers* were read almost as widely in the South as the North (p.38). The Typographic Age witnessed the birth of a unifying information source that need not (yet) worry about outside competition.

Postman also argues that print fosters the rational use of the mind. Furthermore, he states, "It is no accident that the Age of Reason was coexistent with the growth of a print culture (p.51). Indeed, the printed word enables the public to analyze issues and form opinions through the utilization of the rational mind. The print media fostered political debate between candidates running for office. For example, the public was quite interested in listening to the Lincoln-Douglas debates, despite the fact that the debates were lengthy. Each candidate utilized proper grammar and complex sentence

---

† Postman, Neil. *Amusing Ourselves to Death: Public Discourse in the Age of Show Business* (Ch. 4: The Typographic Mind). Penguin Books, 1986, p.51.
* *Ibid.*, Chapter 3.

structure in attempts to persuade the public to vote for him. The structure of these debates was possible only because the printed word encouraged the American public to identify themselves with the English language. If Americans had been unfamiliar with the English language in printed form, they could not have understood the debates. As Postman states, "They [Lincoln and Douglas] consistently drew upon more complex rhetorical sources — sarcasm, irony, paradox, elaborated metaphors, fine distinctions and the exposure of contradiction, none of which would have advanced their respected causes unless the audience was fully aware of the means being employed" (p.47). Evidently, both Lincoln and Douglas respected the intelligence of the American audience.

Another important aspect of the Typographic Age was the public's keen focus on ideas as opposed to physical appearance. The printed word allowed the public to consider what they had read and form logical conclusions based upon the ideas stressed by the print medium. For example, newspapers discussed the ideas of various political candidates so as to inform the public of the major issues at hand at election time. Readers were able to formulate concepts based on what they had read in the papers. Since print monopolized the media industry, the ideas discussed in newspapers served to influence politics tremendously. However, as America moved out of the typographic age and into the "visual" age, *pictures* began to exert a tremendous influence on the minds of the public.

The advent of television was arguably the most important media development since the invention of the printing press. Television provides a unique visual framework for analyzing various aspects of the news. The utilization of television as a medium greatly affected political campaigns. For example, it is commonly accepted that John F. Kennedy won the Presidency due in great part to the fact that the television audience perceived him as good-looking. The physical appearance of candidates began to serve an important role in the political process. Debates previously broadcasted on radio would now be broadcasted on television, where the public could see how the candidates looked. Before the advent of television, Americans were *readers* and *listeners*, but they were never before *viewers* of the news. Instead, Americans had depended on the semantics of the written word to convey meaning. While television provides news in a visual context, the print media requires readers to interpret the news, and form mental images of the actions, people, and events reported in the stories covered.

Television is also the home of major advertisements for political campaigns. While politicians in the Typographic Age respected the intelligence of the American public — as they provided the public with lucid arguments pertaining to vital issues — contemporary politicians utilize the television media to broadcast thirty-second advertisements in which more "candidate bashing" is expressed than actual ideas. For example, close to the recent New York gubernatorial election, New Yorkers were more likely to hear Pataki slander his opponent on short commercials than actually state his views on specific policies. True, there are occasional televised debates between candidates for high political offices, but most political engagement that is broadcast on television is less informative (and thus less useful) than information published by the print media. Unfortunately, as newspaper readership declines, and television viewing continues to dominate the media, many voters are not properly informed about vital political issues.

Television's prodigious influence in contemporary society was examined on an episode of *The Simpsons*. In the episode, Homer was adamant about a particular issue, but then turned on the TV, listened to the opposing view, and, in the midst of being hopelessly confused, said, "TV said *that?* Now I don't know what to think." This satirical line truly demonstrates the impact of television as a conveyor of information to the American public. While Homer will believe anything he hears on television, the message subtly hints that intellectual members of American democracy should not be easily influenced by everything that they hear on television. However, the viewing of good-looking newscasters, and the use of persuasive tones of voice often do have an impact on the minds of many intelligent members of American society.

Despite the advent of new news mediums, the printed word continues to have a strong impact on what news stories are reported to the public. For example, on Sunday mornings, reporters on the television channel *NY 1* buy several papers and actually read selections from the papers during their newscast! Since most of the news reported to the public is thoroughly researched by journalists and newspaper reporters, newspapers continue to serve as the cornerstone of information and news.

In contemporary society, the public does not take a monolithic approach to understanding and interpreting politics in the news. We are fortunate enough to be living in the Information Age, and thus have many opportunities to gather news from various sources. The public has the ability to compare and contrast news from several sources, and then, after reviewing information from all of the sources, formulate informed opinions pertaining to various ideas discussed in the media. While television and the Internet seem to be the wave of the future in terms of news coverage, the public must realize the important contributions of the printed media — both in the Typographic Age as well as in contemporary society.

ESSAY # 2

The Political Television Commercial: A Shift in Political Discourse

"In America, the fundamental metaphor for political discourse is the television commercial."
— *Neil Postman,* Reach Out and Elect Someone

"Vote Quimby. If you were running for mayor, he'd vote for you."
— *Campaign slogan used on a political commercial aired on* The Simpsons

The political television commercial is the symbol of political discourse in the 20th century. The pervasiveness of the television medium enables political commercials to reach a large number of potential voters. For example, Neil Postman notes that "an American who has reached the age of forty will have seen well over one million commercials in his or her lifetime, and has close to another million to go before the first Social Security check arrives" (Postman, p. 126). Since politicians are well aware of the fact that Americans are constantly inundated with commercials, they continue to flood the airwaves with commercials in support of their political campaigns. In an age dominated by visual media, candidates often utilize the insuperable power of television to achieve their personal political goals.

The purpose of political commercials is to *sell* a particular candidate. The role of the politician is to make his audience *believe* he is qualified. In fact, more emphasis is placed on whether a politician appears to be qualified than whether or not he does indeed possess the necessary skills for office. As Postman notes, "what the [political] advertiser needs to know is not what is right about the product, but what is wrong about the buyer" (Postman, p. 128). Instead of stressing political issues, campaign advertisers attempt to find *weaknesses* in the general voting public to secure votes.

Furthermore, Postman correctly states that on television, "the politician does not so much offer the audience an image of himself, as offer himself as an image of the audience" (Postman, p. 134). Politicians have come to realize that they can only sell themselves to potential voters if they appear to possess similar desires as those of the voters. Thus, a good political commercial offers the voting public a portrayal of a candidate as simply an *extension* of the average American voter.

Postman argues that the development of the political television commercial was an inevitable extension of the television medium. The very nature of a visual medium such as television provides viewers with images that in turn engender a strong emotional response. Indeed, political commercials adhere to the adage that a picture says a thousand words. For example, political commercials often show the oppositional candidate in a gray-colored visual framework, while the good candidate is shown in full color (often smiling). Postman's remark that "drama is…preferred over exposition" is certainly true in the televised political sphere. Sixty-second political commercials almost invariably portray one candidate as the "good guy who works hard for the people" and his opponent as "the evil, corrupt politician." Political advertisers and strategists are well in tune with the fact that Americans enjoy competition. In addition, they are aware that human nature dictates that we often choose our "heroes" based on their good deeds, and determine our enemies by means of an analysis of their misdeeds.

Some political commercials that are shorter in length (those that are less than sixty seconds each) often do not have the time to portray one candidate as "good" and the other candidate as "evil." Instead, many political commercials tend to solely portray the oppositional candidate as evil and corrupt. Evidently, political television commercials foster the idea of voting for one candidate by default. In other words, the goal of many marketers is often to knock out one candidate without even considering the ideas of the candidate they are attempting to sell to the voting public. It is often more important for advertisers to create the sense that one candidate is inherently a person composed of poor moral fibers than to actually explain the issues at hand.*

The issue of dissuading voters from voting for a particular candidate was examined (and satirized) on an episode of *The Simpsons*. In the episode, a political commercial pertaining to the upcoming mayoral election was broadcast on the television in the Simpsons' family home. Sideshow Bob's political commercial went as follows: "Is Mayor Quimby a safe choice for Springfield? Mayor Quimby even released Sideshow Bob, a man who has been convicted of attempted murder numerous times, out of prison. Vote Sideshow Bob for mayor." The Simpsonian political commercial provides clear insight into the unique goal of the political marketer, specifically the creation of an unfavorable image of the oppositional candidate. Sure, Sideshow Bob may have attempted to murder several people, but he claims that he wouldn't have allowed a dangerous criminal such as himself out on

---

* *Time* Magazine recently reported that many Democratic presidential hopefuls are basing their election campaigns on their belief that Bush is doing the United States harm. Some may argue that they should spend more time developing their own ideas rather than attacking those of another.

the streets. The commercial is ironic because Bob argues that Quimby presents a danger to society simply because he allowed Bob out of prison! The marketers had the audacity to admit Bob's serious crimes in order to make Quimby even appear even worse.

The fact that the political television commercial has transformed public discourse pertaining to campaign elections may be demonstrated by means of a comparison with the Lincoln-Douglas debates (19th century). The Lincoln-Douglas debates were lengthy (seven to eight hours long), and focused on a concrete discussion of the pertinent issues at hand. Conversely, the political television commercial has enhanced the concept of candidate bashing, as candidates are not provided with adequate time to truly express their ideas on pertinent campaign issues. Still, the shift from tedious public debate to thirty-second visual sound bites still serves to present the same main challenge to candidates: convince the audience *not* to vote for the other candidate.

One fundamental change in political discourse is politicians' perception of the American public. For example, during the Lincoln-Douglas debates, political discourse was based on the belief that the audience was intelligent enough to understand and interpret cogent arguments. As Postman states, "[Lincoln and Douglas] consistently drew upon more complex rhetorical sources- sarcasm, irony, paradox, elaborated metaphors, fine distinctions and the exposure of contradiction, none of which would have advanced their respective causes unless the audience was fully aware of the means being employed" (Postman, p. 47). Both Lincoln and Douglas attempted to secure votes by trying to address the public in a coherent, intelligent manner. Conversely, modern political commercials present an idea to the public in simple terms, so as to not confuse or bore the audience. Postman notes that "today, short and simple messages are preferable to long and complex ones" (Postman, p. 131) Indeed, the television medium is unique in that most of its messages are segmented and do not require much rational thought on the part of the viewer.

Postman also introduces the concept of *disinformation* (Postman, p. 107). Disinformation, which in essence provides potential voters with misleading information, differs from *misinformation*, in which information is by all means false. The danger of disinformation as expressed in political television commercials centers on the sad fact that many viewers believe they are receiving concrete, truthful information when they are actually receiving misleading information directly provided by campaign marketers. The *illusion* of possessing knowledge is perhaps the most dangerous component of the political television commercial. As Postman later notes, "TV does not ban books, it simply displaces them" (Postman, p. 141). Since television commercials create the illusion that they provide knowledge, people often feel they need not turn any further than television as the source for all their political knowledge. Furthermore, disinformation provides an undeniable threat to democracy: in theory, it is better *not* to vote unless a voter has all the facts straight.

Disinformation is perhaps the greatest contributing factor to the establishment of the political television commercial as the most dominant force in modern political discourse. For example, if Americans were simply uninformed, they would have the power to exercise either one of two options: they could either seek more information about campaigns via books or the Internet, or they could not vote altogether. However, since political commercials covertly provide the voting public with disinformation, many, if not most voters are not properly informed as they enter the voting booths.

In dissecting various components of the political television commercial, it is also vital to note the means by which television presents political commercials. One serious consequence of the political television commercial is that Americans have lost their innate ability to *reflect* on new information. Television, by its very nature, is a fast-paced, segmented, loud medium that does not foster rational thought. Instead, dozens of segmented images flash by the screen in a matter of seconds. Once political marketers reach and alter our inner psychological framework, we have little choice but to follow the emotions engendered by political commercials. Furthermore, even if we do choose to search for more information about candidates, our inner psychological states have already been permanently tampered with. For example, if a televised political commercial announces that Bush favors tax cuts for the wealthy, we would certainly remember, if not believe, that idea even if we found additional outside sources denouncing the claim.

Another consequence of the rise of political television commercials as the single most voluminous form of public communication in society centers on the fact that many Americans believe politics can be properly discussed in thirty-second commercials. In reality, thirty-second commercials are targeted at an audience of potential voters who generally believe much of what they hear on television. Consider the "average" man, namely Homer Simpson, and his adherence to television. If television presents itself as an omnipotent, all-knowing power, all other forms of political discourse—such as debate and print media—are deemed irrelevant. Once again, we can clearly see the adverse effects that a single, dominant medium can have on the American public. The core principle of democracy requires that discourse be developed in different mediums and contexts. Thus, the fact that the political television commercial has become such a dominant force in the media industry threatens our cherished perception of democracy.

If we combine each of the aforementioned aspects of political television commercials, we come to the realization that the commercials are a hindrance to democracy. For example, political commercials tend to undermine the democratic principle of *informed consent*. While voters may believe that they are informed about a particular candidate's election platform, they are actually "dis-informed" as a direct result of the disinformation pervasively dispersed in political commercials. Democracy requires voters to possess a tight grasp on campaign issues once they reach the voting booths. However, political commercials tend to concentrate on persuading voters not to vote for a particular candidate—as opposed to openly discussing the issues at hand. If voters often do not give their informed consent pertaining to election platforms at the voting booths, the future of democracy must be placed in question.

ESSAY # 3

Why American Exceptionalism Should Cease to Exist

"Why should I leave America to visit America Junior?"
— *Homer, referring to the Simpson family's trip to Canada*

Throughout American history, Americans have been accused of being selfish. This claim is warranted, since Americans care more about the well being of other Americans than they do about that of non-Americans. Americans have engaged in the principle of *exceptionalism*, viewing themselves as being superior to other people across the globe. After the tragic events of September 11th, many have claimed that we have been witness to a new nation—one of new direction, in which its citizens are wholly committed to creating and maintaining peace throughout the world. According to this argument, American exceptionalism and the Twin Towers collapsed simultaneously. Indeed, we have lost much of our innocence as a result of the attacks. However, the everyday tasks that Americans perform, such as using excess water, demonstrate that exceptionalism is alive and well. Americans believe that they possess certain innate privileges with which non-Americans were not born. Additionally, in matters of terrorism, if we, as a nation, can be targets of terror attacks, we feel that the entire world must have something to fear. In other words, if the United States can be damaged, so can the rest of the world. Americans have no true claim to exceptionalism, as American ideology contradicts the very basis of the principles that we often misinterpret. Americans must realize that despite the fact that America stands as the world's true superpower, we, as a people, cannot feel that we are "better" than non-Americans.

The fact that the United States was built on Lockean theory provides evidence for the argument that we are indeed a selfish nation. As we adhere to Lockean principles, we care only about ourselves, and disregard our neighbors abroad. As for foreign affairs, the general public often argues against intervening in the affairs of other nations. For example, practices of genocide in Bosnia are met with criticism in the United States, but the general public has been hesitant on definitively deciding whether we should involve ourselves in war. Still, when terror struck at home, an overwhelming majority of Americans wanted to exact revenge on the perpetrators of the events. The reason for this is that we care more about ourselves than about other nations. These threads of exceptionalism were exaggerated after the recent attacks; Americans, as Mark Slouka points out, have begun to question their faith.[*] The reason that some Americans questioned their faith only after the September 11th attacks, and not previously during the attacks in Bosnia, lies in the fact that Americans believe that they are exceptional. In adherence to this viewpoint, if something can harm the United States, the world must be coming to an end.

When discussing exceptionalism, the everyday actions that Americans exhibit must be examined. Americans display their belief that they are indeed exceptional by performing simple tasks, such as leaving the water running while brushing their teeth. Despite the fact that we are well aware of the necessity to conserve water, we feel that we are enti-

---

[*] Slouka, Mark. Excerpted in *Harper's Magazine*, Sept. 2002.

tled to use as much water as we want because we are Americans.

Another display of American exceptionalism may be found by examining the consumption of food in the United States. For example, buffet lines at restaurants demonstrate our lack of regard for the starvation problem that plagues many nations. As we read about civilians starving to death in Somalia, we continue to fill our palates with food. Americans know of the problems that plague many nations, and although we might feel sympathetic for other people, we certainly would not sacrifice our own pleasures to help others in need. Americans feel that we have the right to take more food on our plates than we can possibly consume because we are indeed exceptional.

American exceptionalism often manifests itself in arrogance and hypocrisy. For example, as Americans callously leave their faucets running, we silently declare that we have the right to do so because we are Americans. We are arrogant in the sense that we feel that no harm can come to us from the lack of conservation of water in this country. We possess deeply held convictions concerning the conservation of water, but we feel that other people can take care of the problem because they lack exceptionalism. Thus, as we preach about water conservation while simultaneously leaving our own faucets running, we are exhibiting hypocrisy. We feel that our exceptional qualities enable us to do whatever we please, while expecting adherence to strict conservation laws from others. Because America has many resources to spare, we feel that we can make full use of whatever we please, but expect those nations who are underprivileged to conserve the few resources that they have in storage.

What Bart Has to Say

A prime example of American exceptionalism may be discovered through an examination of pop culture. For example, a quote from Bart Simpson, an icon of Americana, cited on an episode of *The Simpsons*, provides clear evidence for American consciousness of superiority. In the episode, Bart asked: "Why would God punish a kid? I mean, an American kid?"[*] For one reason or another, Bart felt that American children are God's favorites. The question posed by Bart Simpson is quite similar to the questions that we asked immediately after September 11th. We have previously seen thousands of children murdered in other nations, yet we suddenly became frightened, questioned our religion, and, for the first time, began to interpret fear as reality once terrorism struck at home. For many Americans, Bart Simpson's question has not been satisfactorily answered.

There are several grounds for why American exceptionalism should cease to exist. Firstly, there are no true qualities that make Americans better than inhabitants of other nations. Many Americans may display great wealth, but we do not perform better in school than other people around the globe. Our educational system is sub-par, and we are taught to grow lazy and feel alienated from our work as we mature into adults[†]. Still, we feel that, despite our shortcomings, Americans are the best people in the world, a chosen[‡] people whose mission it is to hold up the torch of democracy. However, our mission is only important in our minds. Non-democratic nations view democracy as an evil, and each nation is entitled to its own opinion. America's mission is based on superficial grounds, despite the fact that Americans claim to

---

[*] Groening, Matt. *The Simpsons Beyond Forever*, New York: Harper-Collins Publishers, Inc., 2002, p.31.

[†] Mills, C. Wright. *White Collar*. 1951.

[‡] Slouka, Mark. Excerpted in *Harper's Magazine*, Sept. 2002.

have been given the mission by God. American exceptionalism is based solely on principles to which we adhere, and may be dismissed by other nations across the globe. We cannot prove that we have a covenant with God for the same reason that Osama bin Laden cannot prove that America is evil in the eyes of Allah. The true mission of Americans is only held in high regard by Americans, and is disregarded by other nations.

While much of the concept of American exceptionalism is based on religious principles, many Americans have ignored an important quote from the Babylonian Talmud, which serves to dismiss the concept of exceptionalism. The Talmud explicitly states, "Whoever saves a single life...is as if he or she saves the entire world."[*] This religious idea discredits exceptionalism in the sense that the single life referred to in the quote does not explicitly denote a single American life. According to the Talmud, each life is significant, regardless of whether or not the life belongs to that of a chosen person. The Talmud supports an egalitarian viewpoint of people of different cultures. If Americans were to adhere to this view, there would be little resistance to U.S. military intervention in nations that need our support, such as Bosnia and Israel. However, since many Americans are opposed to military action in such areas, they apparently do not value the lives of non-Americans as much as the lives of other Americans. Apparently, Americans do not adhere to religious doctrine that explicitly states the importance of *every* human life, regardless of place of origin.

The United States' Declaration of Independence similarly dissolves the concept of exceptionalism. For example, Jefferson clearly states that "all men are created equal."[†] If Americans truly held to this ideal, we would view non-Americans in a more egalitarian manner. We as Americans would no longer view people from other nations as subordinate. For

---

[*] Babylonian Talmud, *Sanhedrin 37a.*
[†] *The United States Declaration of Independence.* 1776.

example, despite the fact that the United States provided food to Afghan children, many Americans were opposed to the action taken by the government. Rather, many Americans placed the blame for the September 11th terror attacks squarely on the nation called Afghanistan—which included the place of blame on the Afghan people. Still, once the moral fibers of the "average" Afghan person are examined, we can see that their intentions are not to cause us harm. By the amount of protests concerning the delivery of food to Afghanistan, the American public exhibited an extreme lack of regard for non-Americans. As Americans protested, they failed to adhere to the concept of equality amongst all people. As Americans, many of us believe that certain people are not entitled to our charity. Still, if Americans had adhered to the views expressed in the Declaration of Independence, the American public would have been obliged to help those in desperate need of our aid.

Despite the views of those who cannot seem to comprehend the fact that terrorism has struck in America, exceptionalism has not faltered. For example, September 11th has served as a worldwide symbol of terrorism. The events did not merely crush the hearts of Americans; rather, the horrors shook the entire world. Thus, if we are believed to be superior, and we are affected by attacks, the attacks are quite meaningful. The entire world focuses on the September 11th attacks for the simple reason that if terrorists can hit America (the superpower), they can strike anywhere. In contrast, the attacks in Bosnia were viewed as a national symbol of terrorism, as opposed to an international threat to security. No other nation in the modern world could have propagated such international fear as America created after the attacks. Americans are still exceptional in the minds of non-Americans, as the horror of the terror attacks was unable to efface the aura that Americans possess. Americans, now more than ever, overtly exhibit exceptionalism with each wave of the American flag.

ESSAY # 4

The Effects of Industrialization on the Worker: Homer Simpson as the Industrialized Employee

Homer: "Kill my boss? Do I dare live out the American dream?"

Homer: "No, no, no, Lisa. If adults don't like their jobs, they don't go on strike. They just go in every day and do it really half-assed. That's the American Way."

The Industrial Revolution has had a prodigious impact on the worker's way of life. Throughout the course of history, work has played an important role in society. However, the importance of work changed significantly as a direct result of industrialization. A new type of worker was introduced into society, namely, the industrialized employee. In addition, the manner by which work was to be done shifted as a result of new technologies. The characteristics of the factory system have had profound negative effects on the psyche of the worker. Specifically, we can deduce that the former ideal of the work ethic has been replaced by a modern *leisure* ethic.

Since the origin of mankind, work has held special significance in society. A fundamental reason for performing work has been to sustain a living. Work has often served as a means of acquiring wealth. For example, John Locke states "the measure of property nature has [been] well set by the extent of men's labour."[*] In this important statement, Locke introduces the Labor Theory of Value, which claims that labor gives people property, and property creates wealth. Thus, it is possible to deduce that labor invariably makes wealth. Since men are driven by self-interest,[†] they often work very hard in order to obtain great wealth.

Understanding the ideals of capitalism is a vital component in a discussion about the impact of alienation in the industrialized workplace. In the *Wealth of Nations*,[‡] Adam Smith lays down the fundamental components of capitalism. Capitalists strive to earn profits, as profit determines wealth. Capitalists are often ruthless in their methods of obtaining profits. For example, as a result of the industrialization of America, workers were often exploited so as to procure profits for the capitalist. Thus, the concept of greed is a fundamental aspect of capitalism. The greediness of corporate executives, such as those in the Enron scandal[**], as well as factory owners, has had devastating effects on the industrial worker.

The Industrial Revolution altered the industrialized worker's perception of work. Indeed, work continues to serve the purpose of sustaining a living, but industrialized workers feel a sense of *alienation* from their work. Alienation results from workers having no ownership of the means of production, or ownership of the process of production. For example, employees on a factory line do not produce the

---

* Locke, John. *The Second Treatise of Civil Government*. Originally published in 1690. Reprinted by Macmillan Publishing Company, 1952, p.22.

† King, Margaret L. *Western Civilization Volume 2: 1500 - The Present*, 2nd edition. New Jersey: Prentice Hall Inc., 2003, p.442.

‡ Smith, Adam. *The Wealth of Nations*. New York: Random House, 1937.

** Katznelson, Ira. *The Politics of Power: Fourth Edition*. United States: Thomson Learning, 2002, p.153.

entire finished product, and thus do not feel pride in the completed work. In addition, employees do not reap the fruits of their labor, as they are often paid wages or salaries, and thus do not take pride in the finished work. C. Wright Mills describes a former state of work in which the craftsman produced his own goods, was self-employed, and thus took pride in his work.* In fact, Mills cites that from the perspective of the craftsmen, work and play were one and the same. In contrast to this model, the industrialized employee, as a direct result of industrialization, does not feel the same degree of closeness to his work. Rather, he works for the sake of making a living, and does not take a special pride in the product that the factory produces. The finished product is not a reflection of the individual employee's work; rather the product reflects the collective work of multiple employees. The individual employee is not involved in each aspect of producing the finished product, and thus feels separated, or alienated, from his work.

The roots of alienation in the workplace may be examined through an analysis of the historical context of the Industrial Revolution. The Industrial Revolution has created a battle within the workplace. The employer, a capitalist whose goal is to produce a profit, often exploits workers to achieve the corporation's financial goals. For example, historian Norman Ware cites:

"[Workers in Newburyport] are compelled to do all of one-third more work, and in some cases double. Whereas in 1840 the weekly time wages were from 75 cents to 2 dollars per week and board, in 1846 they ran from 55 cents to $1.50, making a 25% reduction in spite of the fact that they were doing 33 percent more work."†

---

* Mills, C. Wright. *White Collar*. England: Oxford University Press, 1951, p. 255.

† Dubofsky, Melvyn. *Industrialization and the American Worker*. Illinois: Harlan Davidson, Inc. 1996, p. 157.

Although the standard of living increased during this period, the average wage of the worker declined. The Industrial Revolution embittered the economic conflict between the employer and employee. In years to come, employers would attempt to use any means necessary to produce a profit.

In the early stages of industrialization, the conditions under which the employee worked were horrific. Employees often worked twelve-hour workdays. Many workers lost hands or fingers from using machinery that they were not properly trained to operate. Child labor was also predominant in the early stages of industrialization. Employees worked for very low wages, as the government did not set a minimum wage. Employers demonstrated their ruthlessness, as their ultimate goal was to produce a profit. Shortly after factory worker H. Dubreuil immigrated to America, he observed the conditions in a machine factory:

> "A wooden structure, cluttered and dusty; machines dating back more than forty years; an uneven and hard earth floor deep in powdered rust that covered your shoes after five minutes of walking; lathe men drowsing over the castings in their machines. I asked myself whether I was in America."[*]

Conditions such as these caused workers to despise work, and inevitably become alienated from their duties.

In the late 1870's, workers collectively expressed their disgust with horrid working conditions and reduction of wages by forming unions. The unions were created in an effort to protect the rights of workers in the workplace. Workers were not satisfied with the conditions under which they worked. As historian Sidney Pollard states, "...the acclimatization of new workers to factory discipline is a task different in kind, at once more subtle and violent, from that of maintaining dis-

---

[*] Dubreuil, H. *Robots or Men?* New York: Harper & Brothers, 1930, pp.62-63.

cipline among a proletarian population of long standing."*
Carleton H. Parker supported this view by theorizing that
the labor movement grew mainly out of the difficulty of
workers in adjusting to factory life.† The unions understood
that employers did not place a high value on the lives of their
workers.

Since the introduction of unions into industrialized society, workers have seen several significant changes in the
workplace. For example, unions have been successful in lob-
bying for a minimum wage. ‡ Still, present work conditions
do not serve to mentally engage workers in their work.
Despite the fact that unions have fought for the rights of
workers and have helped instill a code of ethics in the workplace, many workers are still discontent with their work. For
example, factory worker H. Dubreuil states that employers
"are doing everything possible to disgust the worker with
labor."** While work conditions may have improved over
time, workers are still discontent because of their sense of
"alienation" from their work.

Another core cause of alienation in the psyche of the
industrialized worker lies in the fact that many workers do
not utilize their skills to the fullest extent possible. For example, a worker on a factory line may have a creative mind, but
his thoughts are restricted by the insipid, mundane work of
the factory system. Jean Jacques Rousseau stated that men
should combine their skills in an effort to ameliorate society,
and improve upon what the individual man can accomplish
alone.†† While the factory system allows workers to combine
some degree of their skills, it restricts many of their innate
skills. As Frederick Taylor (the "father of scientific manage-
ment") once stated to an employee, "You are not supposed to

---

* Dubofsky, Melvyn. *Industrialization and the American Worker*, p. 5.
† Horowitz, Irving Louis. *The American Working Class: Prospects for
the 1980's*. New Jersey: Transaction Books, 1979, p.10.
‡ Katznelson, Ira. *The Politics of Power*, p. 95.
** Dubreuil, H. *Robots or Men?* p. 37.

think! There are other people paid for thinking around here."* Obviously, the workplace is not functioning at its full potential since its individual workers are not fulfilling their own personal potential. The restrictions on creativity set by the modern workplace are detrimental to the worker, who will sadly never experience his abilities at maximum potential.

Alienation has had a profound effect on the work ethic of the modern industrialized employee. If we take into context the psyche of the craftsman, we can better understand why the modern employee lacks a work ethic. Craftsmen, as well as other small-entrepreneurs, worked for themselves. The more products they made, the more profit they would obtain. The quality of the work was also important to the craftsman: the better his product was, the higher price he would be able to charge for the item. However, since the industrialized employee is often not directly affected by the quality of his work, he has little reason to work hard. Indeed, the craftsman must perform his work satisfactorily, as he will be fired if he does not do so. However, the industrialized worker performs his work perfunctorily, often with an overt apathy that invariably stems from his boredom.

The former ideal of the work ethic has been replaced by the modern leisure ethic. Mills states, "this replacement has involved a sharp, almost absolute split between work and leisure."† In modern industrialized society (1900-present), leisure serves as a break from the gravity of a job. Employees have lost a sense of freedom in the sense that they no longer freely design what they are to produce. Thus, since employees do not enjoy their work, they have found another means

---

†† Brooklyn College Department of History. *The Shaping of the Modern World from the Enlightenment to the Present: Third Edition.* New York: Simon & Schuster Custom Publishing, 1998. (Rousseau, Jacques. *The Social Contract.*) Reprinted by Hafner Publishing Company, 1947.
* *Ibid*, pp.92-93.
† Mills, C. Wright. *White Collar*, p. 265.

of pleasure—that of leisure. This has shaped the entire realm of global culture. For example, Leo Lowenthal meticulously observed that "the idols of work" have declined, while the "idols of leisure" have risen.[*] The industrialized worker seems to hold more respect for the professional baseball player than the wealthy factory owner. Leisure, which came about as a means of providing pleasure to the employee, has actually replaced the respectability of work. Work is done for the sole purpose of earning a living; pleasure is no longer a notable aspect of work.

The concept of alienation has also brought the worker closer to traditionalist ideals. For example, although the United States remains capitalistic, the effects of industrialization have, with much efficiency, destroyed the principle of a work ethic. Thus, American workers often adhere to traditionalist ideals. For example, a traditionalist, as described by Max Weber[†], would sacrifice money for time. Traditionalists value time with family and friends over profit. As American factory workers opt not to work double-overtime, they are effectively adhering to traditionalist principles. The American employee would rather spend time with his family than perform "meaningless" work because he favors leisure over work. However, the driving force that leads employees to work is that of the acquisition of money. Traditionalists are those individuals who work to live, but do not live to work. Capitalists are those individuals who live to work, and their efforts often produce large profits. The American employee seems to be caught in the middle of these conflicting economic theories. Since the employee despises work so much, he sometimes cannot bear to work overtime. Thus, as a direct result of industrialization, workers often drift away from capitalist concepts, and adhere to traditionalist principles.

---

[*] *Ibid*, p. 265.
[†] Weber, Max. *The Protestant Ethic and the Spirit of Capitalism.* Republished in New York: Scribner's Press, 1958.

One long-term effect of industrialization on the life of the industrialized worker has been his diminished role as an individual. For example, a worker on a factory line may be easily replaced, and thus does not carry a high value with respect to the employer's financial objectives. Because he is easily replaced, his employer does not give him respect, and his value to the corporation is nominal. The functions performed by low-level employees do not require much skill, and factories have experimented with new techniques to reduce expenses. Factory worker H. Dubreuil observes that "great efforts are made to diminish the importance of manual labor."[*] Industrialization continues to diminish the importance of the individual worker, as new technological innovations execute the work formerly performed by workers.

Homer Simpson: The Industrialized Employee

"I'm no longer tyhe money-driven workaholic I once was."

— Homer

The industrialized employee may be exemplified by Homer Simpson. Homer Simpson, the inane safety inspector of the Springfield Nuclear Power plant, feels psychologically alienated from his work. He is employed by the rich capitalist Mr. Burns, who cannot seem to remember Homer's name, even though he has been employed in the power plant for many years. Homer is often seen sleeping at his post, as he is intelligent enough to realize that he will be paid regardless of whether the work he does is satisfactory. In fact, since Homer became safety inspector of the power plant, meltdowns have tripled! While the industrialized employee does need to perform at a certain standard so as to not be fired, he does not

---

[*] *Ibid*, p. 98.

take pride in his work. Homer Simpson is a man who does not enjoy his work, has no interest in the economy, and is eager to spend his time, at home watching television with his family. While his character may be fictitious, the industrialized employee similarly enjoys spending time with his family rather than spending time at work. Homer Simpson, a traditionalist by nature, works to live, but does not by any means live to work. One manufacturer's journal sums up the attitudes of the industrialized worker: "Don't expect work to begin before 9 A.M. or to continue after 3 P.M."[*] Just as Homer Simpson does not "live to work," neither does the real-life industrialized worker.

Homer once exclaimed, "Don't ask me how the economy works!"[†] This line correctly sums up the feelings of the industrialized employee, who accepts his paycheck, spends his money, and does not involve himself in the workings of the economy in any other manner. This viewpoint is contrary to that of the entrepreneur, who was forced to be knowledgeable about the workings of the economy so as to support himself. The industrialized employee does not need to be involved in the inner workings of the economy, as his salary does not depend on his knowledge of any aspect of life outside of his work.

The Industrial Revolution has created the disgruntled industrialized employee. The factory system, which has alienated workers from their work, was created for the sole purpose of maximizing profits. The capitalist employer views the worker as a pawn in the prodigious factory system, and thus cares little about the employee's needs and desires. While the role of the worker may very well change in the future (e.g. due to the effects of automation and other new technologies), the constant function of the worker is to help the employer achieve his specific financial goals. In the process, the worker will earn a small sum of money. Still, given

---

[*] Dubofsky, Melvyn. *Industrialism and the American Worker*, p. 7.
[†] Irwin, William. *The Simpsons and Philosophy: The D'oh! Of Homer.*

the opportunity, the industrialized employee would rather win the money by means of a lottery drawing than by performing his duties at work. And, as Homer has said, "If you really want something in life, you have to work for it. Now quiet, they're about to announce the lottery numbers."

ESSAY # 5:

A CRITICAL EVALUATION OF DESCARTES' MEDITATION I

"The desire to know is innate in humankind."
— *Aristotle, from Metaphysics*

"That whoever is searching after truth must, once in his life, doubt all things; insofar as this is possible."
— *Rene Descartes*

"Facts are meaningless. You could use facts to prove anything that's even remotely true."
— *Homer Simpson*

"I hate quotations. Tell me what you *know*."
— *Ralph Waldo Emerson*

In Descartes' *First Meditation*, Descartes decides to doubt all of his previously held beliefs. He does this because he is a scientist, and concludes that if beliefs can be doubted, then many scientific claims were built on false grounds. Thus, Descartes sets out to build anew from the foundation up (foundational epistemology), and create a house of knowledge where ideas are only allowed entry if they are certain and indubitable (only ideas that meet his standard of knowledge). The lucidity and succinctness of Descartes' three-fold method of doubt enables him to successfully accomplish his task. In *Meditation I*, Descartes' arguments for doubting all previously held beliefs are sound and flawless.

Before Descartes establishes his three-fold method of doubt, he provides a thorough explanation of why certain ideas should not be considered certain and indubitable. In *Meditation I*, Descartes states, "If I am able to find in each one some reason to doubt, this will suffice to justify my rejecting the whole."[*] Descartes explains that it would be nearly impossible for him to explore each aspect of every belief that he holds to be true. Instead, he correctly claims that if one part of a belief cannot be proven to be certain and indubitable, the entire belief must be doubted. For example, if I believe that all apples are sweet, I would not have to try every apple in the world to doubt the belief. Instead, I can attack the *basic principles* upon which my belief rests. In this particular case, I can note that nature sometimes produces fruit and vegetables that have deviant tastes from other members of the same type of food. (I might claim that most oranges are sweet, but have eaten several oranges that were not sweet). Thus, if nature is not perfect, it is impossible for me to believe that every apple in the world is sweet unless I eat every apple in the world. Since this would be quixotic, I have no other choice but to doubt my previously held belief that all apples are sweet.

Descartes then outlines his three-fold method of doubt. Firstly, he argues that much of what we believe to be true was learned through the senses. This leads directly to Descartes' exploration of the *sensory doubt* argument. Descartes claims "it is sometimes proved to me that senses are deceptive, and it is wiser not to trust entirely to any thing by which

---

[*] Descartes, Rene. *Meditations on First Philosophy: Meditation I.*
   Published in 1641. Reprinted: Pojman, Louis P. *Introduction to*
   Philosophy (2nd edition) CA: Wadsworth, 2000, p. 74

we have once been deceived."* Indeed, human beings assume that (for the most part) our senses do not deceive us. However, the senses are *not always* entirely accurate. For example, although I generally place a great deal of confidence in the idea that I hear words correctly, I have had the experience of hearing words incorrectly (especially if my hearing skills were diminished because sounds were out of my normal auditory range). Descartes correctly explains that it is impossible to have complete and utter confidence in our senses. Since senses have occasional lapses in providing the correct information, the data we receive from our senses does not constitute certain and indubitable knowledge. Mike Marlies, in an analysis of Descartes' writings agrees, and asserts: "In fact, 'sense' produces only convincing confusion. Sensations represent nothing, and resemble nothing but one another; they are mere modes of thought."† Even if deception by the senses seems unlikely in a given situation, we can never be absolutely certain that what we perceive is actually non-distorted reality. The sensory doubt argument is flawless because unless the senses provide us with accurate information 100% of the time, we cannot trust the senses entirely.

While a critic of Descartes' sensory doubt argument may concede the idea that perceptions occurring in poor conditions of observation are sometimes inaccurate, he may claim that it is possible to place complete trust in perceptions occurring in more favorable conditions (e.g. the assumption that a person knows that he is performing a particular activity). However, Descartes argues that even perceptions that occur in ideal conditions of observation may be impossible to distinguish from dreams (especially vivid dreams). Descartes outlines the following example to illustrate his point: "...I dreamt that I found myself in this particular place, that I was

---

* *Ibid.*
† Hooker, Michael. *Descartes' Critical and Interpretative Essays.* London: The Johns Hopkins University Press, 1978. (Quoted section: Marlies, Mike: *Doubt, Reason, and Cartesian Theory,* p. 95).

dressed and seated near the fire, whilst in reality I was lying undressed in bed."[*] While his current observations are being made in ideal conditions, there is still no evidence to prove that the observations are absolutely true. In principle, Descartes can be certain of p only if there is no reason to believe that p may be false. Since Descartes has no reason to believe that his current state is not merely a vivid dream, he cannot declare with absolute certainty that he is indeed awake. Since there are no marks to distinguish vivid dreams from reality, Descartes is correct in asserting that it is impossible to be absolutely certain that he is awake at the present moment.

While Descartes' dream doubt argument is very strong and sound, he does insist that he does not "yield too much to distrust, since I am not considering the question of action, but only of knowledge."[†] Thus, Descartes effectively distinguishes between a *theoretical approach* to life, in which he explains that his search is for certain and indubitable knowledge, and a *practical approach* to life, in which he explains that actions need not be hindered merely because they lack the support of absolute concrete knowledge. In asserting this point, Descartes subtly hints at the unique goal of the philosopher: the search for knowledge (often) extended beyond practical purposes. Realistically speaking, it would make no practical difference whether or not I am dreaming at this very moment. Still, from a theoretical (or metaphysical) perspective, it is intriguing to experiment with the notion that reality as we know it may only be perceived reality.

Finally, Descartes introduces the deceitful God (or Evil Genius) argument. Descartes argues that since it is impossible to prove that the world is not run by an Evil Genius (or by a deceitful God), the possibility cannot be ruled out. Instead, we must minimally possess a small amount of doubt pertaining to our perception of reality in the world. Furthermore, the deceitful God argument allows us to doubt whether there

---

[*]   *Ibid*, p. 74
[†]   *Ibid*, p. 76.

is a physical reality at all, and whether simple mathematics constitutes absolute knowledge. (While simple mathematics and the existence of a physical reality both survive the dream doubt argument, they are doubted in the deceitful God argument.) If a deceitful God does actually rule the world, all of our concepts of knowledge pertaining to the world may be considered fabricated perceptions. In other words, if there is an evil force that dominates the world, it may very well deceive us in every aspect of our lives. Of course, it *seems* as though we have physical bodies, and that simple mathematics is concrete, but the *possibility* that we are being deceived is impossible to eliminate. Since we cannot be sure that the world is not ruled by a deceitful being, the opposite belief (that we are ruled by a non-deceitful God) does not constitute knowledge as defined by Descartes' "standard" of knowledge.

An example of the deceitful Evil Genius argument was outlined on an episode of *The Simpsons*.[*] In the episode "Lisa the Skeptic," the townspeople discover a skeleton resembling an angel buried in the dirt. As the episode progresses, there is more and more evidence that serves to reinforce the belief that the skeleton is actually that of an angel. The moment finally arises in which the skeleton speaks to the townspeople and says, "Prepare for the end — the end to high prices! Behold the grand opening of the Heavenly Hills Mall." The angel was voiced by marketers and was simply a publicity stunt utilized by an advertising agency. The issue examined centers on the idea that an outside source can deceive an entire group of people.[*†] In the episode, the advertising agency serves as the Evil Genius that has the ability to deceive people. If an outside marketing source can deceive people, it is plausible to believe that a powerful Evil Genius can likewise deceive people. The deception is noted by Lisa, who succinctly remarks to the marketers: "You played on

---

[*] Richmond, Ray. *The Simpsons: A Complete Guide to Our Favorite Family*. NY: Harper Collins Publications, 1997.

people's innermost fears [an angel that could potentially cause death] just to make a profit." Perhaps the motive of the Evil Genius is to "play with our minds" so as to make "life" into his own game.

In the episode, the townspeople are unshakable in their belief that the skeleton is indeed an angel—until they are proven wrong when the advertisers are revealed as the true source behind the angel mystery. Similarly, while most of us are unwilling to accept the idea that the world is run by a deceitful Evil Genius, we should entertain the idea, as it is not outside the realm of possibility.

In an analysis of Descartes' "rules," Harold Joachim notes that "the ultimate aim of study should be to guide the mind so that it can pass true judgments on all that comes before it."[*] Descartes' mission in *Meditation I* is successfully accomplished: he outlines his standard of knowledge and explicitly asserts why many of our previously held beliefs should be doubted. In outlining this standard, Descartes paves the way for individuals to judge whether or not specific beliefs constitute concrete knowledge.

[†] One exception: Lisa Simpson remained skeptical despite overwhelming evidence that the skeleton was actually an angel. As newsman Kent Brockman asks, "Miss Simpson, how can you maintain your skepticism in spite of the fact that this thing, really, really looks like an angel?"

Similarly, Descartes entertains the idea that an Evil Genius might run the world, and thus is similar to Lisa in that they both question (and may or may not agree with) popular opinion.

Descartes is not considered a skeptic because he later attempts to find the elements that survive his test for knowledge, and uses these elements to construct his house of knowledge. (He finds that a] God exists, and b] he is a thinking thing.)

[*] Joachim, Harold H. *Descartes' Rules for the Direction of the Mind.* London: George Allen & Unwin Ltd., 1957, p. 19.

CONCLUSION

The Simpsons: Content with Being Dysfunctional

If you take only one lesson away from this book, I hope it is the following: Don't you dare mess with *The Simpsons*. Sure, they're "dysfunctional," but that's certainly no reason to ridicule them. (In fact, as Homer would probably say in regards to comments made about his family: you can't spell 'dysfunctional' without 'functional.') Barbara Bush and William Bennett learned that lesson the hard way. Barbara Bush, for example, once remarked "*The Simpsons* is the dumbest thing I've ever seen."[*] She later apologized for the comment. (Bennett also had his qualms with *The Simpsons*, only to later retract a disparaging statement that he had made). As mentioned earlier, the elder President Bush also made a disparaging statement about *The Simpsons*, only to be criticized by Bart on an episode that aired three days later. The writers of *The Simpsons* aren't afraid of anyone—even the head of Newscorp (the parent company of Fox):

---

[*] Pinsky, Mark I. *The Gospel According to The Simpsons*. Kentucky: Westminster John Knox Press, 2001.

Homer: Hit the road, gramps! This is a private skybox!
Rupert: I'm Rupert Murdoch, the billionaire tyrant, and
　　this is my skybox.
　　　　　　　　　　　　　　　　　　　－ *"Sunday, Cruddy Sunday"*

I'd also like the reader to realize that while *The Simpsons* may not be able to focus on every important issue prevalent in contemporary society, they do focus on a great number of vital issues that are relevant in our society.

The Simpson family may not be the ideal family in American society. However, the family is a fairly accurate (although satirized) depiction of the average American family in contemporary culture. Not every family is perfect, and the Simpson family certainly encompasses the flaws that plague many real American families. Most families in American society are not perfect. Instead, they have real problems: problems pertaining to ethics, morality, financial status, and family unity. While the Simpson family has many of the same problems that real American families face in our daily lives, and thus can be considered simply a reflection of family life in America, the family truly possesses a keen influence on one important aspect of our family life—that being unity within the classic familial structure. As I have shown, the Simpson family is extremely tight-knit. In fact, during the several instances in which the family seems to move farther apart from each other, episodes invariably conclude with the Simpson familial unit intact. (Recall "Barting Over," the episode in which Bart moves out of the Simpson house, but ends up moving back in with the family by the conclusion of the episode). Familial values are inherent to the very nature of the Simpson family. While the family may be dysfunctional, the family members are satisfied with their lives, and possess true love for one another. To emphasize this important point, please note the following song that the family sang during the Shary Bobbins episode:

Homer: Around the house, I never lift a finger.
              As a husband and father, I'm sub par.
              I'd rather drink a beer
              than win Father of the Year.
              I'm happy with things the way they are.
Lisa: I'm getting used to never getting noticed.
Bart: I'm stuck here till I can steal a car.
Marge: The house is still a mess,
              and I'm going bald from stress —
Bart and Lisa: but we're happy just the way we are.
Flanders: They're not perfect, but the Lord says "Love
              thy neighbor."
Homer: Shut up, Flanders.
Flanders: Okely, dokely do.
Shary Bobbins: Don't think it's sour grapes,
              but you're all a bunch of apes.
              And so I must be leaving you.*

The Simpson family teaches us that it doesn't really matter what other people think of you as long as you're happy with who you are as an individual (or in this case, as a familial unit). Indeed, avid fans will jump up out of their seats and remind themselves of the following quote said by Homer that would serve to contradict the aforementioned point: "Son, being popular is the most important thing in the world." Given this quote, we can take away the following: Homer believes that he cares about what other people think of him. However, by declaring that "he'd rather drink a beer than win Father of the Year," he effectively dismisses any claim that he cares about the ways in which people perceive him. Instead of considering such matters, Homer would probably rather drink a Duff beer. Homer also teaches his children that popularity is not all that important. When Bart works for Krusty, for example, Bart's classmates don't

---

* Clausen, Alf. *The Simpsons Songbook*. United States: Warner Brothers Publications, 2002.

believe him. Homer tells him: "Don't worry about what a bunch of fourth graders think. You're doing what you want with your life."

All in all, the Simpson family is a genuinely decent family. They work as a team to survive the struggles of daily life. They also enjoy being together: it is no accident that the family sits together on the living room couch before each episode begins. The family values togetherness—even though they themselves may not realize it. In the end, fans come to the realization that the Simpson family is just like their own family. In great creative works, it is often difficult to determine whether the work is simply a reflection of society or whether society is a reflection of the work (kind of like the famous chicken and the egg conundrum). While there are certainly many ways in which *The Simpsons* influences society (as outlined in this book), it is sometimes difficult to tell whether the series is a reflection of our own existence, or whether our society is merely a reflection of Simpsonian society. At some point, we come to the following conclusion: the two societies are one and the same. And before you frown, stop and think for a moment. Think about all of the aspects of Simpsonian society that are vital in our lives—from politics to education to healthcare. Then challenge yourself to pick out the character on the series who most defines who you are (everyone IS essentially a Simpson!). Forget your previous role models: Michael Jordan, the Fonz, Stephen Hawking, Bill Gates... nah...the *Simpsons* character you have just chosen, my friend, is essentially your American idol. (My favorite character on the series is Homer Simpson. Homer once remarked that we're all a little bit like him: "You can't depend on me all your life. You have to learn that there's a little Homer Simpson in all of us.")

So now you've reached the end of this book. I suppose you have better books to read anyway. May I suggest Homer's *Odyssey*?

Homer: "Homer's Odyssey? Is that about the time I bought that minivan?"

And finally, in the words of Homer J. Simpson, "That's my cue to exit."

Unless otherwise noted, all quotes found in this book were found in the sources listed in the bibliography, or directly from the episodes via my own memory. I have made every attempt possible to find exact word-for-word quotes, but several quotes have been paraphrased. I can assure readers that any minor changes in the wording of specific quotes have not changed the meaning behind the quotes. Similarly, readers may occasionally find slight alterations of plot situations within this book. I apologize in advance for any slight (and accidental) modifications of *Simpsons* episodes discussed in this book.

BIBLIOGRAPHY

Websites/ Published Web Articles:

The Simpsons Archive (www.snpp.com) for quotes, plot summaries, and an excerpt from Ed Bishop of *The Riverfront Times.*

Interview with Matt Groening:
http://www.snpp.com/other/interviews/groening93.html

BBC Simpsons polls:
http://newsvote.bbc.co.uk/1/hi/programmes/wtwta/2959462.stm
http://news.bbc.co.uk/1/hi/entertainment/tv_and_radio/2984426.stm

Many of Homer's quotes were found at:
http://www.angelfire.com/comics/pearly/homer/homer-quotes1.html

Bart's Prank Phone Calls:
http://moes.virtualave.net%2Fpranks.html

American medicine quotation found at:
http://www.snpp.com/other/papers/bv.paper.html

Idato, Michael. "Ready, set, d'oh!" February 27, 2003
http://www.smh.com.au/articles/2003/02/26/1046064102384.html

The Cosby Show quotes: http://www.imdb.com/Quotes?0086687

Bush's speech on the war with Iraq:
    http://www.atour.com/government/usa/20030116b.html

Batman quote website:
    http://www.geocities.com/cicatrix_zero/batman.html

Books:

Aristotle. *Metaphysics.*

Babylonian Talmud, *Sanhedrin 37a.*

Brooklyn College Department of History. *The Shaping of the Modern World from the Enlightenment to the Present: Third Edition.* New York: Simon & Schuster Custom Publishing, 1998. (Rousseau, Jacques. *The Social Contract.*) Reprinted by Hafner Publishing Company, 1947.

Clausen, Alf. *The Simpsons Songbook.* United States: Warner Brothers Publications, 2002.

Descartes, Rene. *Meditations on First Philosophy: Meditation I,* 1641. Reprinted: Pojman, Louis P. *Introduction to Philosophy (2nd edition)* CA: Wadsworth, 2000.

Dubofsky, Melvyn. *Industrialization and the American Worker.* Illinois: Harlan Davidson, Inc. 1996.

Dubreuil, H. *Robots or Men?* New York: Harper & Brothers, 1930.

Gimple, Scott M. *The Simpsons Forever: A Complete Guide to Our Favorite Family Continued.* New York: Harper Perennial Publications, 1999.

Hooker, Michael. *Descartes' Critical and Interpretative Essays.* London: The Johns Hopkins University Press, 1978. (Quoted Section: Marlies, Mike: Doubt, Reason, and Cartesian Theory).

Irwin, William. *The Simpsons and Philosophy: The D'oh! Of Homer.* Illinois: Carus Publishing Co., 2001.

Joachim, Harold H. *Descartes' Rules for the Direction of the Mind.* London: George Allen & Unwin Ltd., 1957.

Katznelson, Ira. *The Politics of Power: Fourth Edition*. United States: Thomson Learning, 2002.

King, Margaret L. *Western Civilization – Volume 2: 1500 - The Present (2ⁿᵈ edition)*. New Jersey: Prentice Hall Inc., 2003.

Locke, John. *The Second Treatise of Civil Government*. Originally published in 1690. Reprinted by Macmillan Publishing Company,1952.

McCann, Jesse L. *The Simpsons Beyond Forever: A Complete Guide to Our Favorite Family Still Continued*. New York: Perennial, 2002.

Mills, C. Wright. *White Collar*. England: Oxford University Press, 1951.

Pinsky, Mark I. *The Gospel According to The Simpsons*. Kentucky: Westminster John Knox Press, 2001.

Postman, Neil. *Amusing Ourselves to Death: Public Discourse in the Age of Show Business* (Ch. 4: The Typographic Mind). Penguin Books, 1986.

Richmond, Ray. *The Simpsons: A Complete Guide to Our Favorite Family*. NY: Harper Collins Publications, 1997.

Smith, Adam. *The Wealth of Nations*. New York: Random House, 1937.

Terrace, Vincent. *Television Sitcom Fact Book*. United States: McFarland & Company, Inc., Publishers, 2000.

Weber, Max. *The Protestant Ethic and the Spirit of Capitalism*. Republished in New York: Scribner's Press, 1958.

Published Articles (Non-Web):

Slouka, Mark. Excerpted in *Harper's Magazine*, Sept. 2002.

Solomon, Michael. *"They're Yellow, But They're Not Chicken."* TV Guide: Feb. 15-21, 2003, p.27.

MacGregor, Jeff. *"More Than Sight Gags and Subversive Satire."* Review. New York *Times*, 20 June 1999: Television/Radio 27

Documents:

The United States Declaration of Independence. 1776.

TV References:

The Tonight Show with Jay Leno
The Late Show with David Letterman
Family Guy
Roseanne
I Love Lucy
The Flintstones
The Honeymooners
Leave it to Beaver
Married With Children
The Tracy Ullman Show
Batman
Teenage Mutant Ninja Turtles
Popeye
Superman

Movie References:

Patch Adams

A SPECIAL MESSAGE TO MY NUCLEAR FAMILY

"As far as anyone knows, we're a nice, normal family."
— *Homer J. Simpson*

Mom, Dad, and Justin: You have always encouraged me to pursue my goals. I'm sure you didn't think watching *The Simpsons* would amount to anything, but alas, here's a book based on America's favorite family. Despite the fact that *The Simpsons* are America's favorite family, the three of you comprise my favorite family. And don't think for a moment that I didn't have each of you in mind while writing this book:

Mom: It's hard to pin down what you've given me in just a few words. To say that you've always been there for me is clearly an understatement. We're a lot alike – except when it comes to M&Ms. (Next time I buy a bag, I'll save you the brown ones, but the green ones are mine). Also, *The Simpsons* is better than *I Love Lucy*. I promised myself that I wouldn't reveal in this book that your real hair color isn't blue (oops).

Dad: Well, I can't say that you're like Homer. For one thing, you're smart. Secondly, you don't drink beer. Still, you've been known to eat your fair share of donuts, given the chance. Thank you for your encouragement, and for always being there to talk to. Don't take a second job at the Kwik-E-Mart.

Justin: You're as smart as Lisa. We've spent countless hours watching *The Simpsons*, and discussing quotes from the show. It'd be easy to say that I keep you around just so you could give me quotes to use in my book, but that's not the case. You're a really cool guy, and I'm lucky to have such a great brother. Thanks for keeping down that "infernal racket" while I wrote this book.

ACKNOWLEDGMENTS

I'd also like to acknowledge the following groups and individuals:

My grandfather, Poppy Leon, with whom I speak about national and international politics, play chess, and always learn a lot; Nana, who taught me how to bake rugelach, and with whom I have shared many good times; my grandmother, Florence, who has always supported everything I have attempted; my other family members, with whom I've spent many fun times.

My close friend John, who co-founded Backrow Inc, and with whom I have engaged in countless conversations about *The Simpsons*; Daniel, who has been one of my closest friends since high school; Dmitriy, who has been one of my closest friends, despite the fact that he doesn't think *The Simpsons* are the "shiznit"; my basketball buddies; my friends in the CUNY Honors College; my friends in college campuses across the United States; Dr. Duncan Dobbelman for his invaluable advice; the editors of *The Excelsior*; my friends in the Brooklyn College student body; my friends and co-workers in the BC Learning Center; *The Simpsons* Archive, for their wealth of resource material; and every other Simpsons fan across the globe.

I'd also like to thank Hats Off Books, and my editor, Summer Mullins, for her great work.

ABOUT THE AUTHOR

Steven Keslowitz is a University Scholar in the CUNY Honors College at Brooklyn College. He is currently employed as a Writing Tutor and Greek/Roman Classics Tutor in the Brooklyn College Learning Center. He also writes for the Brooklyn College Newspaper, *The Excelsior*. He was named a winner in two national essay contests (Kaplun 2000, 2002 contests). He has declared a political science major, and plans to pursue a career as a lawyer.

Mr. Keslowitz also hopes to follow his true dream of becoming the safety inspector of the Springfield Nuclear Power Plant. In his spare time, he enjoys drinking Duff beer at Moe's Tavern. He has made a guest appearance on the Itchy and Scratchy show, in which he provided the voice for Poochie, the rockin' dog. He is also full of neighborly love ("Shut up, Flanders").

Printed in the United States
17654LVS00001B/319-369